Colossians

Shirley Hamilton

Contents:

Preface   9

Introduction   11

Colossians Chapter One   15

Colossians Chapter two   101

Colossians Chapter Three   175

Colossians Chapter Four   251

Preface

The book of Colossians is full of warmth and love from the beloved apostle who is writing to the churches of Jesus Christ from his last prison cell.

I have chosen to write about this book, as I wrote a commentary on the letter to the Ephesians some years ago, and this letter is similar in many ways, and full of Christian teaching which was relevant in my life at the time. Recovering from trauma is difficult but with our eyes on Christ, we will be overcomers.

As I have written my comments in this commentary, I have relied deeply on the work of the Holy Spirit in my mind and heart and have checked my understandings and interpretations with authors such as John Calvin, John Gill and Matthew Henry. I am indebted to these men of faith and deep insight to support my own interpretation and insight.

It is my hope that God will bless you as you read this devotional commentary and that your understanding of the Lord will be helped and deepened.

Introduction

The letter to the church at Colosse was written by the Apostle Paul in AD 62. The church at Colosse was founded by Epaphras who became a Christian in Ephesus, and planted the church in Colosse, seeing the need there. The letter is addressed to the holy people in the church at Colosse. It was the smallest church to whom Paul wrote an Epistle. Colosse suffered a massive earthquake two years after this letter was written and the city was destroyed.

Paul begins the letter with thanksgiving to God for the believers in Colosse and extends warm love to them. His prayer is that they make progress in the faith and in love for their Saviour, Jesus.

"For this cause, we also, since the day we heard this, don't cease praying and making requests for you, that you may be filled with the knowledge of his will in all spiritual wisdom and understanding, that you may walk worthily of the Lord, to please him in all respects, bearing fruit in every good work, and increasing in the knowledge of God; strengthened with all

power, according to the might of his glory, for all endurance and perseverance with joy; giving thanks to the Father, who made us fit to be partakers of the inheritance of the saints in light; who delivered us out of the power of darkness, and translated us into the Kingdom of the Son of his love; in whom we have our redemption, the forgiveness of our sins;"

Colossians 1:9-13

The preoccupation in this letter is the person of the Lord Jesus Christ. The supremacy of Christ is paramount in the mind of the Apostle Paul, and he addresses difficulties that the church is having and encourages them in the faith handed down to him by God and preached and taught by him as the Apostle to the Gentiles.

Paul focuses on the person and work of Christ; the message of the gospel; dealing with false doctrine; focus on Christ in the Christian life; prayer.

Paul writes this letter from a prison cell, his last prison cell. He is still concerned about the churches of Christ and writes to them and cares for them, right to the last moment of his life. He is alone except for Luke and asked for others to visit him, even Mark, who was rejected in the past. He is cold and asks for his cloak and the books and parchments that he has in Ephesus. His protege Timothy is to bring them to him and bring the comfort he needs at this time.

This Epistle is for the edification of the church at Colosse and also us who read it now. It points our view and our mindset to the Lord Jesus Christ and His pre-eminence in our lives. It takes our view away from ourselves and the pagan and distracting religion that is everywhere in all times and cultures and puts our focus on the LORD.

I hope this series of writings will be an encouragement to you as a Christian and if you are not a Christian, that you will fix your mind on Christ and come to Him as the only Saviour of our soul and He who holds our eternal destiny in His hands.

Colossians Chapter One

29 verses

V1 introduction

"Paul, an apostle of Christ Jesus through the will of God, and Timothy our brother,"

Paul starts his letter with his spiritual credentials. Paul does not boast about his academic qualities or qualifications but values his Apostleship above all. He is an Apostle of Jesus Christ, one born out of time and through the will of God.

He includes Timothy his beloved younger brother, who he has trained up in the ministry and is dependable and faithful to the Lord. The Colossians knew Timothy, and this would add weight to the Epistle and encourage them to listen to what the Apostle said to them for their spiritual benefit.

The believers at Colosse had never seen Paul in the flesh and therefore he endears himself to them, that they might listen to the Apostle that God has provided for them, to encourage them in the Lord their God and in their faith in the Lord Jesus Christ.

Paul has the weight of the will and authority of God behind what he is saying here in this letter and has been made an Apostle and is validated by the Word of God, which he preaches and teaches. All his authority, doctrine and miracles of validation come from God and are validated in the Holy Scripture.

V2 Grace

"to the saints and faithful brothers in Christ at Colosse: Grace to you and peace from God our Father, and the Lord Jesus Christ."

Paul addresses the Christian believers as *"saints and faithful brothers in Christ."* This is the faithful and true band of believers in the church at Colosse, who love the Lord Jesus and have true faith in Him. This is a typical salutation of the Apostle Paul.

He sends them grace and peace from God the Father. To know the grace of God is to be a possessor of salvation and the forgiveness of sins in the Lord Jesus Christ. All those who possess this grace are the redeemed people of God who have that peace with Him, and all punishment and condemnation has gone for them. To have peace with God, is everlasting peace and precludes all peace. There is no peace if we have no peace with God.

"Who gave himself for us, that he might redeem us from all iniquity, and purify for himself a people for his own possession, zealous for good works."   Titus 2:14

To know the Lord Jesus Christ is the greatest state to be in, for in Him, we have peace with God and with all others. He is our peace and has bought this situation for us with His precious blood.

"But now in Christ Jesus you who once were far off are made near in the blood of Christ. For he is our peace, who made both one, and broke down the middle wall of separation,"

Ephesians 2:13-14

Without Christ we are far away, but now are brought near and enjoy the fellowship of His Holy Spirit and the company of other believers. Paul addresses the saints at Colosse and also all of us who love Christ and belong to the kingdom.

V3 Thankful

"We give thanks to God the Father of our Lord Jesus Christ, praying always for you,"

How good to be thankful for Christian fellowship and the spread of the gospel. Paul is thankful to God for these sisters and brothers in Christ, even though he has never met them, and probably will never meet them. They are precious to him because of the link with Epaphras, who became a Christian believer in Ephesus and saw the need for the Christian witness in Colosse, and started the church there. Paul is supportive of his brother, who has been a trailblazer in this regard. He writes to encourage him and the congregation that he leads.

Paul is thankful to God for His saving power displayed in the church at Colosse and is glad for the blessing on this church. He knows that God leads people as He sees fit and will expand the cause of Christ through many and varied witnesses. Paul gives his blessing in this cause for the Lord and assures them of his prayers.

We tend to think of the churches praying for Paul in all his travelling and ministry, but Paul shows us the necessity for the

Pastors and Teachers to pray for their own people and Christians in other settings too. Paul is the great Apostle, and his prayers are heard in heaven, as a faithful and righteous man.

"Confess your offences to one another, and pray for one another, that you may be healed. The insistent prayer of a righteous person is powerfully effective."

James 5:16

V4 Love

"Because we have heard about your faith in Christ Jesus and your love for all the saints..."

Paul gives thanks to the Lord and prays for these true believes, because he has heard about their faith in the Lord Jesus and that they love each other as well. Paul knows how they are trusting in Christ and leaning upon Him for protection and rescue and have committed their souls to Him for salvation and heaven. Perhaps he has had conversations with Epaphras and has had discussions about the church and the difficulties it faces as a body of believers. Epaphras was a spiritually minded brother, who also ended up in prison like the Apostle Paul. Paul is writing to encourage them all in the Lord Jesus their Saviour and to help them to have full confidence in Him alone.

This love is the mark of the true Christian, and it is the seal that will keep the Christian in the love of God right to the very end of their lives and the end of the era. Many make the claim to be Christians in our time but this mark of the Spirit in not in their lives. Many claim to be

Christians and have no feeling for other people, not even the people of God. This should not be. We can boast of our faith and can boast of our great works for God, but if there is no love for other believers, and love for those without a Saviour, we have not the love of God in our hearts and minds.

"I saw, and behold, the Lamb standing on Mount Zion, and with him a number, one hundred forty-four thousand, having his name, and the name of his Father, written on their foreheads."

Revelation 14:1

Christians are sealed with the Holy Spirit and kept safe until that great day of the marriage supper of the Lamb. We exhibit the fruits of the Holy Spirit who indwells the lives of the people of God and the greatest of these is Love.

"Beloved, let us love one another, for love is of God; and everyone who loves is born of God, and knows God."

1 John 4:7

"I heard the number of those who were sealed, one hundred forty-four thousand,

sealed out of every tribe of the children of Israel:"

Revelation 7:4

We do not love in word only but in deeds and acts of kindness and support for each other. To neglect each other is to not love, and we are not made perfect in love. These saints in Colosse were not like that, but prayed, sympathised with and served each other, as they saw need.

V5 Hope

"because of the hope which is laid up for you in the heavens, of which you heard before in the word of the truth of the Good News,"

The faith and love of the believers at the church in Colosse is secure because their eyes are firmly on the coming kingdom. Their hope in Christ is real and certain, because they believe. They consider what God has laid up for them in the coming kingdom and it influences every part of their lives, in faith and love.

"Rejoice, and be exceedingly glad, for great is your reward in heaven."

Matthew 5:12

This is the key to Christian contentment. Whatever state we are in, nothing and no one will touch our eternal inheritance kept in heaven for us. It is the constant comfort and confirmed in us by the Holy Spirit. The things of this life never completely satisfy us, and our souls need something beyond us to fulfil our spiritual desires.

The Colossian Christians heard this truth in the preaching of the gospel. They heard this from Paul's teaching and also

Epaphras, and Paul is reminding them of this truth. The element of the eternal must be part, the main part of the gospel, otherwise it becomes a social gospel and therefore no gospel at all. If there is nothing beyond the here and now, then nothing is worth it.

"If we have only hoped in Christ in this life, we are of all men most pitiable."

1 Corinthians 15:19

The main event is after this life, and what an event it will be! As we lay hold of the gospel of truth, that those who are forgiven and believe have a glorious treasure laid up for them in the heavens, so we will persevere to the end and our salvation will last the test of time in this difficult world.

Beloved, whatever you are facing, keep your faith and love alive and hold on to the glorious hope in Christ of the coming kingdom. It is the good news of the gospel of Jesus Christ and the power of God to salvation, to everyone who believes.

V6 Fruit

"…which has come to you; even as it is in all the world and is bearing fruit and growing, as it does in you also, since the day you heard and knew the grace of God in truth;"

The truth and good news of the gospel has come to the Christians at Colosse through the will of God and the labour of Epaphras. He has been given a heart of deep feeling for the people of Colosse and longs to see them brought to God. He has started the mission there, after his own conversion at Ephesus. Paul knows Epaphras and is supporting the work of God at Colosse, because he knows Epaphras will be faithful to the gospel that is being spread everywhere.

The good news that Jesus is the Saviour of human souls is spreading and the kingdom is being set up in this world. As the message is preached, people are being touched by the Holy Spirit and seeing their need of forgiveness and therefore coming to faith in Christ. It is a wonderful time of gathering in souls for the kingdom of God.

Trouble is coming, even for this little church in Colosse. They will need this letter from the Apostle Paul to support them in the coming days. An earthquake is coming which will destroy Colosse and the church will be affected, maybe closed, or maybe the Christians will be spread further abroad. It is often hard to understand the purposes of God, but they are sure and steadfast, and His will is not thwarted by anyone. God will honour the work of Epaphras and encourage him in his faith. He is a faithful servant and spends time in prison like the Apostle Paul. Paul describes him as a fellow-soldier in the faith.

The fruit of the gospel is spreading everywhere and taking root and bearing more fruit. This is true in the lives of the believers at Colosse too. They are growing in grace and faith and love, since the time they heard and believed. They are making good progress in the spiritual life and are growing in numbers and in the knowledge of God and in His particular love for them. They serve Christ and each other as they live their lives devoted to God.

V7 Worker

"…even as you learned of Epaphras our beloved fellow servant, who is a faithful servant of Christ on our behalf,"

Again, Epaphras is commended to the Colossian Christians as a *"fellow servant"* and a *"faithful servant."* Epaphras is faithful to his Lord and God and has a heart for the people and for the spread of the gospel.

Paul not only counts his brother in Christ as faithful, but also a fellow servant. Paul is the Apostle to the Gentiles but sees himself as a humble servant of God. He does not Lord it over others or presume that they want to listen to him. He counts himself as the least of believers, because he persecuted the church of Christ and is "one born out of season"

"And last of all — as to the untimely birth — he appeared also to me, for I am the least of the apostles, who am not worthy to be called an apostle, because I did persecute the Assembly of God"

1 Corinthians 15:8-9

The witness of Paul to us is huge, not just in what he has said, recorded for us in Scripture, but in the magnitude of the holiness of his life.

Although Epaphras is not an Apostle, Paul counts him as acting and speaking on his behalf, as the leader of the congregation. Epaphras has taught the Colossians Christians the gospel and has carried out the will of God in that place.

V8 Sharing

"And who also informed us of your love in the Spirit."

Epaphras talks to the Apostle about the church at Colosse and gives him information about their practical and spiritual state. He shares the situation in the church with the Apostle and involves him because the knows that Paul is interested in the spiritual welfare of the congregation and Epaphras seeks further teaching and encouragement for them.

Paul is struck by the love of the people in the Spirit of God. There is really no love without the Spirit and Paul understands the outworking of the Holy Spirit in the lives of the believers at Colosse because of the reports he gets from Epaphras. This is striking in that their love is obvious to Paul even though he has never met them.

Beloved, does our reputation for love go before us? Do people see that we love the people of God and the souls of those who are lost? Our hearts should be drawn to sisters and brothers in Christ and also to those who need the Lord in salvation. Love is the defining mark of the Christian, and it should be obvious to those who know the Lord themselves and those who do not.

Our greatest love is for the Lord Jesus and His word, and we treasure Him above all things.

V9 Wisdom

"For this reason, since the day we heard about you, we have not stopped praying for you and asking God to fill you with the knowledge of His will in all spiritual wisdom and understanding,"

Because of the love in the souls of the Colossian Christians, Paul is almost overwhelmed for them and prays continually for them. The things he asks for in their regard are spiritual things. He asks that they are filled with the knowledge of the will of God for their lives. This can be a very difficult thing to work out, as we can get confused about what we want and what God wants for us. We can ask for guidance and have our own agenda already worked out! We must come to God humbly and ask for His purposes to be worked out in our lives and not just what we think is best.

Sometimes God's purposes for us are just to accept the present circumstances and be glad for the provision of the Lord in our lives at that particular time. He has promised never to leave us and will keep us safe in Him to the end and bring us safely home to heaven. We seek to be holy and blameless before Him and work out our salvation with the fear of God and wishing never to disappoint Him. His will for us is to be holy and to live upright lives in all our many and varied circumstances. The details of our lives will be worked out by the Lord, and He will direct our footsteps along the pathway to knowing Him better. Then we will be more adept at discerning what His will for us is and what is best.

"I will instruct you and teach you in the way which you shall go. I will counsel you with my eye on you."

Psalm 32:8

"...and the LORD will guide you continually, satisfy your soul in dry places, and make your bones strong. You will be like a watered garden, and like a spring of water whose waters don't fail."

Isaiah 58:11

This is also the spiritual wisdom and understanding that Paul talks about. It is good to be wise towards God and not in the ways of this vain world. We search the Scriptures for understanding and knowledge and apply the principle of godly living to our thoughts and behaviour. To have wisdom is the greatest thing and we seek it from God every day.

V10 Worthy

"That you may walk worthily of the Lord, to please him in all respects, bearing fruit in every good work, and increasing in the knowledge of God."

The Christian walking with God through life is an ongoing and interactive activity. It is not just something that the Holy Spirit does in us, but we grow as we obey Him and learn from Him. We put a guard on all our behaviour and speaking. We watch ourselves and keep short accounts with God. We engage with the Word of God and prayer. This was the desire of Paul as he wrote this letter to the Christians at Colosse.

Paul asks them to walk worthy of the Lord, that means to live godly and holy lives that reflect the goodness and perfections of the Lord. He tells them they should live to please the Lord in all areas of their lives and so should we. No area is out of bounds to the Lord, but all is brought into subjection to Him and His commandments. As we learn from the Holy Spirit, we conform all our ways to His ways and obey Him. We become more like the Lord our

God and make progress in holiness. This is the purpose of the Christian life.

"Acquaint yourself with him, now, and be at peace. By it, good will come to you."

Job 22:21

As we follow the Lord, we will meet all that is good for us, and it will do us earthly and eternal good. We have good in our lives because the Lord is merciful to us and encourages us in all our desires to follow Him. We should be bearing fruit in every good work and prospering in all areas of our mind and soul. Our knowledge of God will increase as we walk with Him and obey Him as he directs our footsteps each and every day. As we put to death the desires of our fleshly lives, we will progress to increasingly spiritual understanding and obedience to the Lord. If we pander to our flesh, it hurts our spiritual life, and we find ourselves floundering in the murky waters of temptation and selfishness.

Beloved, do not let the sinful flesh separate you from knowing the Lord better and drawing closer to Him. Do the things that cause us to bear fruit and walk with the Lord in our daily lives. Keep up our spiritual duties and fight the sin that so easily entangles us.

"Therefore let us also, seeing we are surrounded by so great a cloud of witnesses, lay aside every weight and the sin which so easily entangles us, and let us run with patience the race that is set before us, looking to Jesus, the author and perfecter of faith, who for the joy that was set before him endured the cross, despising its shame, and has sat down at the right hand of the throne of God."

Hebrews 12:1-2

V11 Power

"Strengthened with all power, according to the might of his glory, for all endurance and perseverance with joy;"

Christians live their lives strengthened by all the power of God. This brings victorious Christian living. We have the full power of God at our disposal, yet we fail and falter and are not over comers. We allow the sinful mindset of the flesh to infiltrate our thinking and the vain philosophies of the day to dictate how we think and process our situation. This makes us weak because we do not rely on the word of God but on the foolishness of human thinking.

The rise of psychology is also a factor in the way we think and process our daily lives. We take up these issues so easily from the media and our education and forget the promises and statutes of the Lord. The Scripture is sufficient, but we add to it and allow the worldly way of thinking into our psyche. This effects how we process our difficulties, and we can forget to bring them to God, who is ever ready to help us.

The might of the glory of God is ours, yet we do not possess it or live in the light of it. We find it hard to take in, how the glory of God can be in our lives and the power of the Holy Spirit to take us and fill our lives with His joy. He can give us the power to endure all things and to persevere in our Christian lives right to the end. This is the mark of the true Christian, the one who truly knows God and belongs to Him only.

This joy of the Holy Spirit in not necessarily an outward expression of emotion, but an inner peace. It is a deep well of inner calm and happiness that cannot be touched by the things of this life. It is from God and is therefore something that He bestows on His people who love Him and are faithful to Him. It is a deep and silent power that enervates the Christian to be holy, for God is holy.

"Then he said to them, "Go your way. Eat the fat, drink the sweet, and send portions to him for whom nothing is prepared; for this day is holy to our Lord. Don't be grieved; for the joy of the LORD is your strength."

Nehemiah 8:10

We do not need to be cast down by our circumstances, but we can rely on the Lord to sustain us in the trials and give us peace and contentment, even in the middle of great trauma. The Lord is real and to know Him is real, and we lay hold on His great and precious promises to sustain us and fill us with this joy. As we read His word we can be overcome with a sense of our own weakness and unworthiness, and we can feel we are not sufficient. We are not sufficient, that is the point! The Lord is willing and able to sustain us and when we need forgiveness, he is always there, ready to forgive and restore us to close fellowship with Him. His loving kindness is extraordinary and when we experience it, we are filled with the joy of the Lord.

It is curious that we do not have the steadiness and constancy in our lives when the strength of the living God is available to us. Too many earthly considerations get in the way of our daily walk with God, and we do not know the Word of God sufficiently to apply it in our daily lives. We forget so quickly what we have heard and read and revert to the earthly ways of thinking and processing.

Beloved, let us grid up the strength of our mind and soul and give ourselves to the Lord today. We rest on that glorious joy that comes from the power of the Holy Spirit within us, not of our own making, but of His eternal purposes. We will endure and persevere under His personal and powerful work in our lives.

V12 Partakers

"...giving thanks to the Father, who made us fit to be partakers of the inheritance of the saints in light;"

For all the spiritual blessings we enjoy as the people of God, we give God the ultimate praise and glory. We give thanks for our free and sure salvation that has been purchased for us by a Saviour's blood through the death of Jesus on the cross at Calvary. Because of what he has opened for us, we are partakers of the glorious inheritance of the saints in light. It is not just a home in heaven, but we are actually made heirs of God and joint heirs with Christ to the throne of heaven and the eternal kingdom.

"The Spirit himself testifies with our spirit that we are children of God; and if children, then heirs; heirs of God, and joint heirs with Christ; if indeed we suffer with him, that we may also be glorified with him."

Romans 8:16-17

We are made fit through Christ, through the imparting to us of His righteousness, for we have none of our own. He took or sins and paid for them and has given us his own goodness so that we are made righteous, really righteous, before a holy God. We rest under the wings of His protection and saving love.

Paul seeks to show the Christians at Colosse the full glory of the Saviour Jesus and what he has done for them. It is too easy to let this slip and to take the message and the provision for granted. We have an enemy who would seek to dull our view of the excellency that is in Christ and to undermine our outlook on what He has done and what he means to us as Christian people. We have no inheritance apart from Him and no standing before the holy God, the Father.

The fatherly love of God has secured this blessing for us in Christ and looks on us as dearly beloved children. We are no longer children of wrath, but our adoption into the family of God, makes us rightful heirs to the kingdom and we will rule with Christ in that kingdom. The kingdom is all light and the light of God now shines on our hearts because of Jesus. We stay away from the kingdom of darkness and the unfruitful works of evil and lift up our

Saviour with thanksgiving always to the LORD.

"For you were once darkness, but now you are light in the Lord. Walk as children of light, for the fruit of the light consists in all goodness, righteousness, and truth. Test and prove what pleases the Lord. Have no fellowship with the fruitless deeds of darkness, but rather expose them."

Ephesians 5:8-11

V13 Translated

"...who delivered us out of the power of darkness, and translated us into the Kingdom of the Son of his love;"

God our Father in heaven has delivered us. He has rescued us from the powers of darkness and given us light.

The word *"translated"* in this verse of the Scripture means to take from one place and put in another. We are taken out of the kingdom of darkness and put into the kingdom of light. It is a work of God and no one else could do such a thing, certainly not ourselves! It is a translation from one kingdom of darkness to the other kingdom, of light. It is a complete change of position and situation and location. We go from lostness to being found. We turn from evil to embrace the righteous. We are destined for heaven and not for hell.

We are delivered from our natural, sinful, state of being, because we are trapped and cannot save ourselves. The bonds of death have taken hold of our souls and we cannot get free. We are doomed to die the second death and we need a Saviour to free us from our bondage. Only Jesus can do this and only the complete Godhead has power and inclination to do it. We are set free by the merit of Christ and the will of God and the power of the Holy Spirit.

Darkness has no more hold over the Christian because of what God has done for us. We become children of the light and become members of the kingdom of the Lord Jesus Christ, indeed, members of His body. More, we are daughters and sons of the kingdom and heirs with Christ as His redeemed people. What we have been saved from is dire and what we are saved to is glorious in the extreme!

"… seeing it is God who said, "Light will shine out of darkness," who has shone in our hearts to give the light of the knowledge of the glory of God in the face of Jesus Christ."

2 Corinthians 4:6

Jesus the Saviour, is the *"Son of his love."* The Father has entered into a covenant with the Son, to redeem us from sin for Himself and to set us free. The Father loves the Son, for they have always been together and always will be. The Son is precious to the Father, and it required all the love of God towards ignoble us to set in motion redemptions plan. The Father gave up His one and only Son to death, to be able to forgive us and make us righteous. This was the cost of Him dying for us, and our only appropriate response is gratitude. This is why Christian's love Jesus so much. This is the reason the Father loves the Son, for He is the beautiful One, the one who sacrificed Himself for the sake of His people, that we will be with Him forever in the eternal kingdom.

Beloved, let us never forget who we once were and who we are now. We are the gift of God to the Son, as the people of His kingdom. We are the bride that waits for the Bridegroom, and will enjoy the wedding supper of the Lamb, in the place prepared for us.

"For you have delivered my soul from death, and prevented my feet from falling, that I may walk before God in the light of the living."

Psalm 56:13

V14 Redemption

"In whom we have our redemption, the forgiveness of our sins;"

In the Lord Jesus Christ we receive all the blessings of God, because we are redeemed people. In our natural state we are dead in sin and slaves to its in-dwelling power and influence in our lives and souls. It keeps us dead to God and living under the condemnation of the death of our soul, the second death. It is like being a slave locked up indefinitely, with no freedom and no rights. We cannot free our own soul because it is dead to God and without the working of the Holy Spirit in our minds and hearts, we have no desire for God.

"For as many as are of the works of the law are under the curse; for it is written, "Cursed is everyone who does not continue in all things which are written in the book of the law, to do them." But that no one is justified by the law in the sight of God is evident, for "the just shall live by faith."

Galatians 3:10-11

Christ came to redeem us from this curse, which is the curse of the holy law of God who cannot look on unrighteousness and we are therefore outcasts and rejected from the coming kingdom. We live our days under the fear of death and the condemnation of eternal punishment. Jesus came into this world as our Saviour and paid the dreadful price of our unrighteousness, so that we could be set free from this spiritual slavery.

He can really set us free! He is our loving Saviour and will be the Lord of our lives to guide us and keep us for eternity. The cost to set us free was huge - the death of our Saviour, but He rose again for our sake. He can forgive the sin which holds us in the slavery and set us free from it totally. We can have the victory through Christ who died and rose again, and forever lives for us. It is a real freedom, and we can now choose not to sin rather than be its slave.

"Stand firm therefore in the liberty by which Christ has made us free, and don't be entangled again with a yoke of bondage."

Galatians 5:1

Just like a slave can be redeemed from the slave market, so we can be "bought" out of the state of sin that we are in and made righteous people. We are bought with that shed blood of Christ, which saves and can keep us and set us free.

V15 Firstborn

"Who is the image of the invisible God, the firstborn of all creation."

The Lord Jesus Christ is the image of the invisible God. He is the image of God revealed to us in human flesh. He came to rescue us from a dying world and set us free from the tyranny of sin. He shows us God because He is in all His being God, but also revealed in the mortal flesh that He forever bears on our behalf. He shows us the character of God and the being of God in His majesty, power and revealed dignity in the God/man. We see God in the flesh, and we see the thoughts and deeds and speech of God as Jesus walked this world and interacted with us. He is Emmanuel "God with us."

He is the uncreated one and so is the firstborn of the creation, His existence is before time and has always been. He is the eternal Son of the Father. He was there at the creation of the world, indeed is called the Creator who is to be forever praised. Everything that exists is His and has been made by Him, and all things have their being to serve and worship Him.

"In the beginning was the Word, and the Word was with God, and the Word was God. The same was in the beginning with God. All things were made through him. Without him was not anything made that has been made."

John 1:1-3

Jesus is the eternal word and is exalted high above all the creation as its Lord and God. We worship Him as such and love Him with all our minds and hearts and souls. There is no other response that we can give to such a one as He, who has shown us the way to God and how to walk worthy of the Lord.

Jesus is also the firstborn of the dead. He has been raised for our justification and the proof that He is who He says He is. One day we also will rise, because He is risen for us. He lives forever as the Lord of life and the conqueror of all death.

"And from Jesus Christ, the faithful witness, the firstborn of the dead, and the ruler of the kings of the earth. To him who loves us, and washed us from our sins by his blood;"

Revelation 1:5

The Lord Jesus comes first in all things, for He has humbled Himself and become obedient to God the Father, even to the death He suffered on the cross. He is the first and the last, the beginning and the end.

V16 Dominion

"For in Him all things were created, things in heaven and on earth, visible and invisible, whether thrones or dominions or rulers or authorities. All things were created through Him and for Him."

Again, the Apostle Paul reiterates the depths of the truth about the Lord Jesus Christ. All things were created in Him according to His express authority - things that are material and things that are spiritual. The visible things that we see in the physical world, and the things that are invisible to us, the thrones and power and dominion and authority in the heavenly realms, are all created by Christ, and according to His purposes. He has created all the things and they are for Himself. He alone is the maker and sustainer of the worlds, the seen world and the unseen world.

Many are foolish and do not even see the work of Christ in the beauty of the revealed created order. They imagine it was all an event that happened for no reason and came from a chance beginning, from a state of nothing - it just happened. This is illogical and foolish to think that something that exists can come out of nothing! Christ has always been there as the eternal Son, but many seek to deny His existence and so make up stories about the way things are and how they came about in the past. We must not be duped by it and led away into the realms of the unreasonable and illogical.

If we cannot believe what we see as being from Christ and God, then what about what we don't see. Many have a vested interest in unbelief in the unseen world of the Spirit so that they can escape the authority of the Lord over them and their lives. They explain away the created order as a happy accident, and that the spiritual realm is just fairy tales. Everyone knows that that is not true, but the desire to escape the over-arching authority of God, causes many to swallow falsehood and lies and irrational thinking.

"...Because knowing God, they didn't glorify him as God, and didn't give thanks, but became vain in their reasoning, and their senseless heart was darkened. Professing themselves to be wise, they became fools,"   Romans 1:21-22

Romans chapter one explains the reasoning behind the mind of God against those who try to explain Him away and escape the logic of His reason. We become foolish when we refuse to believe what God clearly tells us and what we know as the witness in our own hearts.

All things were made for the glory of the Lord Jesus, including us, but we have become so foolish that we refuse Him. We refuse His authority over us and become ungrateful for His blessings in our lives and descend into unbelief. Our hearts harden and we refuse the message of God and become people without God and without hope in this world.

"See that you don't refuse him who speaks. For if they didn't escape when they refused him who warned on the Earth, how much more will we not escape who turn away from him who warns from heaven,"

Hebrews 12:25

Beloved, do not even listen to the lies in your own heart. Trust the Word of God and the power of reason He has given you. Do not pander to your own agenda of refusal and seek the Lord today. The Lord

Jesus will have all the pre-eminence as He is the Lord of everything that exists. This is good for us, for He is also the Lord of love and seeks to bring us into His kingdom, if we would believe. If only we could see Him as He truly is, and we can, for He is revealed here, in this verse in all His splendour and glory.

Jesus, who is over all thrones, dominions, rulers and authorities and orchestrates the whole of history for the glory of the Father and the salvation of His people. We rejoice to know Him, who we love, for He has first loved us and given Himself for us. He is willing to bless us and shower us with all spiritual blessings, if we would but come to Him and give ourselves to Him.

V17 Before

"He is before all things, and in him all things are held together."

When there was no world, no universe and no human life, there was the Lord Jesus Christ, in the bosom of the Father, the Eternal Son of the only God, the Creator of all things.

His existence is before time - in eternity and forever settled. He has no beginning and has no end. He is the second person of the godhead and is the Saviour of our world. He made all things that exist and upholds them all by the word of His mouth. He holds all this together and all things exist and consist because of Him. He is the great Creator, and nothing exists in earth, heaven or eternity that He did not make.

He creates by the word He speaks. What He wills into being, exists and lives.

This is the God we believe in and serve. He is the high and exalted one, far above all and the only God that exists. Yet, in such humility, has humbled himself to associate with us in our misery and grief and deliver us from the powers of darkness and bring us into the kingdom of the Son.

"God, having in the past spoken to the fathers through the prophets at many times and in various ways, has at the end of these days spoken to us by his Son, whom he appointed heir of all things, through whom also he made the worlds. His Son is the radiance of his glory, the very image of his substance, and upholding all things by the word of his power, who, when he had by himself purified us of our sins, sat down on the right hand of the Majesty on high…"

Hebrews 1:1-3

Jesus is the invisible God, made visible in human flesh and has become our Saviour and Lord. He has kept us in His love by the power of the Holy Spirit and through the blood shed for us on Calvary's cross. He is able to save the least and the lowest, and though the eternal God, loves sinners and eats with them. He is the humble Lord with the most loving heart, that rules the universe, heaven and all powers, with no harshness or vindictiveness. This is the God we serve…

V18 Pre-eminence

"And He is the head of the body, the church; He is the beginning and firstborn from among the dead, so that in all things He may have pre-eminence."

In all things, our Lord Jesus Christ has the preeminent place. He is the Alpha and Omega, the beginning and the end, and no one can overtake Him or displace Him. The Lord of love is still on the throne and always will be. We can be full of confidence that he will overcome all evil finally and forever and bring His waiting people home to heaven to fulfil all things and finalise the kingdom of God.

The people of God are the Church of God, the group of people who belong to Him because of what he has done for them. They have believed in Him and put all their trust in what He did on the cross and are forgiven and justified by His mercy and grace alone. The Church are the redeemed people of God, bought out of the sinful way of life by the precious blood of Christ and made right with God. The Lord Jesus Christ is the head of that Church, which is His body, and He will bring His people out of this world and out of the grave and into the life eternal with Him forever. Christ alone has the authority over the Church, and He decides our lives and future according to His tender mercies and glorious power.

Christ Jesus is the first fruits from the dead, for He has risen to bring about the kingdom of God and show that He is the Lord of life and all the Church. He is not just the first from the dead but is the one who raises people from the dead, as He did when He was here on earth. If Jesus had not been raised from the dead, then neither would these people have been raised. He raised Himself to restore all things which were lost when humankind fell in the garden and lost their standing with God. Jesus was the commencement of the kingdom of God and so is the beginning of that mighty body of believers and kingdom of saints.

He raised people by His mighty power and gave life to dead bodies, and so is the Lord of physical life. He is also the Lord of spiritual life and is the one who gives life to the soul and raises the soul to a resurrection of faith and love in Him. The supremacy in all things belong to Christ because he has made all things and upholds all things. He also restores the things that have fallen away and subjects them to His authority. All honour is due to Him.

V19   Fulness

"For all the fullness was pleased to dwell in him;"

Not only does the Lord Jesus have the pre-eminence in all things but He is the fullness of God, and the fullness of God dwells in Him. The fullness of God is all righteousness, power, authority, wisdom and every spiritual blessing, and so it abides in our Saviour Christ. God gives this position to the Son that the glory of God might be revealed to us and all the created order, in this world and other worlds. The whole of heaven will bow to the Son, and He will reign for ever and ever. The people of God will reign with Him in all glory and power and dominion. This is the Lord we serve and the future of the saints of God.

All our righteousness and our future blessings depend on Christ. We look to Him only and see the fullness of the Father God and rejoice that we belong to Him. Only in Him are we safe and secure and in faith we trust in Him to bring us safely home to heaven and lead us through this tempestuous life to the safe haven of our spiritual home.

"I am the vine. You are the branches. He who remains in me, and I in him, the same bears much fruit, for apart from me you can do nothing."

John 15:5

Without the power of God in our lives we will remain impotent to serve the Lord and will not persevere to the end of our lives with The Lord. We will eventually fall away and cease from our spiritual life and become darkened once more.

Beloved, how much we need the Lord and how great is our dependence on Him. Let us strive to enter into the joy of walking with Him every day and keeping our pathway pure and right with God.

If we should detract from the Lord Jesus and fail to see and render to Him His due place in our lives, we undermine our salvation and detract from the truth of God. This is not a feature in the life of the true believer, and so we give Him all the glory due to Him and stick closely to His word and not the word of another.

Those who love the Lord are humble and walk that way with Him. We will bring many to righteousness by our quiet and godly living and in the way we interact with others.

"True instruction was in his mouth, and nothing false was found on his lips. He walked with Me in peace and uprightness, and he turned many from iniquity."

Malachi 2:6

We emulate the pattern of the Lord Jesus and how He conducted Himself as He walked this sinful world. We also should be like Him, and know Him as our close companion, that we might please Him and honour Him for who He is.

V20 Reconcile

"...and through Him to reconcile to Himself all things, whether things on earth or things in heaven, by making peace through the blood of His cross."

Here is the crux of the matter. Peace with God comes at the highest, most costly price - the death of the Lord Jesus in the midst of such suffering as He bore the penalty for our personal sin. His blood was spilt so we would never have to suffer the guilt, blame and eternal punishment for our crimes. The shed blood satisfied the demands of the law of God, that sinful people could be free to be righteous and perfect before God. The perfect Saviour, Jesus, pays the ultimate price for our failure and loss. Such is the love of the holy God. Jesus died and made the peace between the holy God and our sinful selves. He paid the price that the law of God required for the penalty of our sin. There is no peace with God apart from this.

We are alienated from God and dead in trespasses and sins, yet we can be made alive again and we can be reconciled to God through what Jesus did for us. This is the greatest deed anyone has ever done for anyone else! We can never really take it in, because it is just too great and too amazing. The fact that Jesus did what He did is beyond our human comprehension, and we can only try to think of it and remember Him and be so thankful. It is indeed, love poured out and the greatest expression of love there has ever been or will be.

God the Father has sent the Son to be a reconciliation for us and to redeem us from sin. We can enjoy the peace of God because of this and soon we will enjoy that peace continually and deeply in the kingdom.

But more. Jesus reconciled all things to God, in heaven and on earth. The whole creation is groaning, waiting for the final consummation of the kingdom of God so that it will also be delivered from the bondage of death. The whole of the created order waits to be released from the bonds of sin and be at peace. The end of the striving for existence and significance, is the beginning of a kingdom where justice and peace reign.

"That the creation itself also will be delivered from the bondage of decay into

the liberty of the glory of the children of God. For we know that the whole creation groans and travails in pain together until now."

Romans 8:21-22

Jesus brings peace to us on earth and also brings peace in heaven. Bringing peace in heaven involves the keeping of the holy angels beyond the possibility of falling or failing and being free totally from the destroying power and effect of sin. Some of the angels fell and became evil, and those who remain are now made righteous and cannot fall. They do not need forgiveness, since they never rebelled, but the death of Jesus also reconciled their situation to God and secured their eternal state before God.

God becomes our Father rather than our judge and we rejoice in him and His provision for us.

V21 Past times

"You, being in past times alienated and enemies in your mind in your evil works,"

We have great need of this reconciliation with God, because of our moral and spiritual state before Him. We are His enemies and alienated from Him because of the state of our mind and the evil works that come from that state. We are the enemies of God because our minds are not conformed to His ways of thinking, and we have a warped and faulty mindset that leads us and keeps us away for knowing God and walking with Him.

Paul is reminding the believers in Colosse of the dire state of their previous life without the Lord and the evil mindset that they once had. This has all been changed now because of Christ and what He has done for them. They are reconciled now through the shed blood of Christ, and He alone is able to rescue them from sin and keep them in right fellowship with the Father.

The mindset is changed when we come to God. We take on the humble state of being contrite before the Lord and are changed by God and brought to repentance and faith because of Him. We are no longer puffed up in the pride of our own thinking, but take on ourselves the mind of Christ, who has shown us the way to God. We see His mind, His words and deeds as He lived here on earth, and we read the record of them in the New Testament. We understand how we must relate to God, and we walk in obedience to that way.

The redeemed person is no longer an enemy of God, but a dearly beloved daughter or son and brought into a right relationship with the Father and in the family of God. The evil works have now dealt with, and we are walking in fellowship with the one who made us and loves us with unending love.

It is good to remember who we once were and what we have now been given in Christ. He has rescued us from the empty way of life we once had and given us dignity and purpose in His dearly beloved Son, so that now we also are dearly beloved children and saints of God. What a salvation we possess and what a Saviour that He should include us in His kingdom!

We now have a renewed mind, and our speaking and deeds are free to be conformed to His image and we are able to please him because of our faith in Him.

V22 Blameless

"yet now he has reconciled in the body of his flesh through death, to present you holy and without blemish and blameless before him,"

Christ has to come in the flesh to deal with the sins of our flesh. He willingly took on the body of His humanity and went through the process of birth and growth as a human man in order to identify with us and be the representative of the human, who would make recompense to God for our sin. He willingly walked this sinful world, that we might have a pattern for life and a model to live by. He sacrificed His life in heaven to walk the road of suffering in our world. How difficult it must have been for Him to live here as the perfect man amid the sea of fallen and sinful people in our society.

Yet in his body He bore away the punishment for our sin and reconciled us to God. He paid the dreadful penalty for our sin so that we would never have to. The price was the death of that precious and perfect body, that He took so willingly on our behalf. It was so bruised and battered that you could not see the features of His face and it was so broken,

Jesus could not carry the cross to the site of crucifixion. We will never understand the depths of such a love, until eternity. We have no love like this, we are such rotten creatures, who have killed our Saviour on the cross and caused Him to suffer so.

Because of what He suffered and the price He paid for our sins, the physical and spiritual price of it, we get to go free. This is the greatest news the world has ever heard, and yet we are so silent about it. Are we ashamed about it? Has it become commonplace to us in our minds? We really need to consider Him regularly and meet with other believers around the table of remembrance, so that we never lose sight of what was done for us and accomplished on that cruel cross.

We were presented to God as holy people, without any stain of sin on us and with all our acknowledged blame firmly put away, through the sacrifice of Christ. Blame is such a destructive emotion and brings us down if we believe what other people tell us. Although we have done wrong things, yet the effect of the blood of the covenant secures our position before God and we are made righteous before Him. We are not faultless as Christians, but made blameless before Him in love.

"... *even as he chose us in him before the foundation of the world, that we would be holy and without blemish before him in love;*"

Ephesians 1:4

We are free people, free from any condemnation and free to choose to do the right thing and love God first and best. We will seek to be like Him and to serve Him with everything we are.

V23 Steadfast

"if it is so that you continue in the faith, grounded and steadfast, and not moved away from the hope of the Good News which you heard, which is being proclaimed in all creation under heaven; of which I, Paul, was made a servant."

These deep and great provisions made for us by God are ours and are the reality of our lives if we continue in the faith. We have the call to persevere to the end and make our salvation a reality. We must endure many things and keep close to the Word of God and make our calling and election sure.

"But he who endures to the end, the same will be saved."

Matthew 23:13

We must be grounded and steadfast if we are to endure to the end of the road. The road is long and full of temptations and dangers and if we are to be over-comers, we must ground ourselves in the Word of God and remain committed to following the Lord Jesus. We rejoice to read the Scriptures every day and meditate on the precepts and put them into practice in our lives. The Scripture is the only foundation for our faith and life, and we must not deviate from it or look for other sources of teaching and comfort. God is our teacher and the Spirit within will direct our thoughts and give us good motivations to obey and serve. He will give us the grace to persevere and continue safely to the heavenly home and the full fruition of our salvation.

Our hope for the future is in the gospel of Jesus Christ. There is no other message of salvation and no other means whereby we can come to God. The truth about the coming kingdom and the promise of complete salvation from our sin and a hope in heaven is our hope, not the things of this life. Even the reality of Christian fellowship is not the ultimate comfort to us, but the fact that we are included in the kingdom and will one day be with Christ and reign with Him. Our union with Christ is everything and powers and enervates all we do and is our motivation for life and service.

This gospel is still being proclaimed and beloved by all who are marked for salvation. The message of the gospel is being spread through the whole earth and we keep it free from the contamination of falsehood and false "Christian" religion. We keep to the message revealed in the Scripture and handed down to us from the Apostles. It is easy to contaminate the message, but God will keep His people and ensure all who will come to Him will be saved. There is much falsehood today and so many voices that preach and teach and call us to listen. We must be discerning about what we listen to and judge correctly about what is from the Word of God and what is not.

Paul is a servant in this regard and has laid down his life to spread and guard this message of the gospel so that many will be saved and come to know Christ. God has set Him apart to do this and this is the calling of all those who know the Lord Jesus, to spread the good news and rejoice in the forgiveness of sins. We continue to search the Scriptures to fill our minds with the truth of it, so that our discernment will grow and our courage to stand for the truth is strong. God will honour us if we put Him first and keep the message of the gospel true to His revealed Word and obey Him. Then our hope will be sure and steadfast, and we will endure to the end.

V24 Afflictions

"Now I rejoice in my sufferings for your sake, and fill up on my part that which is lacking of the afflictions of Christ in my flesh for his body's sake, which is the assembly;"

Paul is rejoicing in the fact that his sufferings are his fellowship with Christ and for the edification of the church. Paul is not the Saviour of the church but the one who builds it up and strengthens the believers to follow the Lord and only Him. Paul is an Apostle, and his words are recorded in holy Scripture for our benefit as the people of God. This letter is not just for the lifting up and instruction of the Christians at Colosse, but for the whole, the Church of Jesus Christ. It is the Word of God.

The Apostle Paul rejoices to be counted worthy to suffer with Christ and to bear in his body the marks of that suffering. He speaks about making up the sufferings of Christ in his own body, as if he is fully identifying with the suffering Saviour. Christ suffered for us and bears in His body, the scars that show how he suffered and the consequences of our sin. We rejoice in those sufferings of the Suffering Saviour, for they bought our freedom and released us from the penalty of our sins, the eternal death. It is not a shame to suffer for Christ, to be misunderstood and treated in a cruel way, as this is the pathway of every Christian. We do not "fit" the way of this present evil age, as our minds have been renewed and our souls are alive to God. The evil around us grieves us, because we belong to God and the Spirit who dwells within us witnesses with our spirit that we are children of the heavenly kingdom.

As we progress in the Christian life, the ways of this world become less and less attractive to us as the Holy Spirit refines our lives. Part of this is the road of suffering, and God permits us to suffer that we might lean heavily on Him and trust in the words that He says to us.

It is becoming increasingly hard to be part of anything in this world, as the corruption of sin spreads wider and becomes more virulent. It is affecting even the church of Christ and points to the coming end times. We need to be always on our guard about what we put into our minds and what we tolerate in our behaviour. God wants all of us, body, soul and mind, because He knows that is what is best for us. In the time of suffering, we will look to Him and find that He is all we need. We too will identify with Christ and be full of joy to be counted worthy to suffer for His sake.

V25 Stewardship

"… of which I was made a servant, according to the stewardship of God which was given me toward you, to fulfil the word of God,"

Paul may have been the apostle to the Gentiles, but he regards himself as a servant of the church. He does not lord it over the Christians or think highly of himself. He is a servant of Christ, who has been given a task to do by God, which he is accountable for. He has been given the task and the message that he is preaching, according to the will of God that the Word of God might be fulfilled.

Paul takes his position very seriously and has suffered much because of it. He is very earnest to be a good steward of the task in hand and to fulfil all the word of God, as to what God requires of him. He is a minister of the church and a preacher of the gospel. These two tasks go hand in hand, for the message of the gospel must go out if people are to be saved.

The message is powerful and effectual and can bring souls to a place of belief in God and lives of power and service.

"For I am not ashamed of the Good News of Christ, for it is the power of God for salvation for everyone who believes; for the Jew first, and also for the Greek."

Romans 1:18

Paul's dedication to the cause of Christ to the Gentiles people, is seen in this book so clearly. He lifts up the Lord Jesus that we might see Him clearly and what He has done for us, which is the whole purpose of the life of Paul, and the life of every Christian. The more clearly we see Christ, the greater our devotion. The more clearly the gospel is preached, the greater the spiritual harvest of souls.

Paul is investing his time well and laying up his treasure in heaven. It certainly is not in this world! He is a good steward of his life, for he is investing it in the purposes and ways of the Lord his God and not in himself. Our stewardship of our time and effort should be patterned after the example of Paul, and we also will bear spiritual fruit to God.

V26 Revealed

".. the mystery, which has been hidden for ages and generations. But now it has been revealed to his saints,"

The mystery of the Word of God is the message of the gospel. The Word is God proclaims the gospel in the Old and New testaments and has been revealed from the beginning. But it is veiled in the time before Christ. It is held for the Israelite nation and entrusted to their care for the time of great understanding when it would be proclaimed to all people and revealed to the saints of God. The message can only be understood and accepted when the Holy Spirit gives the person discernment to accept it and believe. It is by the mercy of the Lord that we have this message and the power to believe it.

The Word in the New Testament is the clear and open revelation of Jesus Christ to the world. He is presented as the Saviour of the world and the Holy Spirit is given freely to all who repent and believe. The full light of God shines out in the message of the gospel and the way to God is made plain and so easy for the fallen human psyche to access and follow. The gospel message rings out from the Scripture and the faithful voices that preach it, and we can hear and believe.

At the appointed time and generation, Jesus comes into the world and ministers to us and shows us the heart and mind of the Father. He shows us the standard of God; teaches us the way to God and gives His life as a ransom for many. Christ raises up servants who will proclaim the good news about salvation and a new life for all who come to Him in faith. The way is opened up to the Gentile nations as well as the Jewish nation and the message goes out to whoever will listen. In the generations past it seemed that the Gentile nations were left out of the reckoning of God and the way was darkened for them, but now the light has dawned, and the message is open to whoever wants to listen and believe.

"Many nations will go and say, "Come, and let us go up to the mountain of the LORD, and to the house of the God of Jacob; and he will teach us of his ways, and we will walk in his paths." For out of Zion will go forth the law, and the word of the LORD from Jerusalem;"   Micah 4:2

Salvation is offered freely and there are great gatherings into the kingdom, of people to faith in Christ, and the Christian pathway with God. The kingdom has come, and God is calling in His elect people who will bow their knee to Him, obey, and follow the way of Christ.

The way to God is now revealed and the hidden message is now the message being preached to all. It is revealed and understood by the saints of God and all who believe in the Lord Jesus are brought into fellowship with God, with renewed minds and heart of love.

"It will happen afterward, that I will pour out my Spirit on all flesh; and your sons and your daughters will prophesy. Your old men will dream dreams. Your young men will see visions. And also on the servants and on the handmaids in those days, I will pour out my Spirit."

Joel 2:28-29

What a glory to be alive in these days! What blessings we enjoy and what possibilities for those who believe! Let us take our place as the servants of the Lord and proclaim the good news however we are able, in all our circumstances and with great joy. Let us not be bowed down by our situation and the difficulties of life and the discouragement of the enemy. The Word is revealed, and we believe, by His mercy alone...

V27 Riches

"…to whom God was pleased to make known what are the riches of the glory of this mystery among the Gentiles, which is Christ in you, the hope of glory;"

The saints of God are now identified as including the Gentile people, of whom the Colossian Christians are a part. God does not just include the Gentile nations but makes known to them the richness of His glory. All the glory that is revealed in Scripture is now revealed to all who will come to God in faith. The offer stands to the "whosever will" and all humankind is now invited to hear and respond to the gospel message.

The mystery of the gospel has now been revealed to all peoples. The door of mercy is open to all who will respond to the gospel call and repent and believe. All that has been kept with the Jewish people, is now fully open and available to anyone who seeks the Lord. The glory of God is that He has lifted the Gentiles, who have dwelt in darkness for so long, and are now included in the church of Jesus Christ. It is the mystery and crown of the magnificent gospel message.

Anyone can respond and enjoy the riches of salvation: forgiveness of sin; a new life in Christ; spiritual communion with the eternal God. This caused quite a stir with the Jewish believers, who did not want to give up their exclusive relationship with God, and God has had to deal with His people to show them the riches and depths of his mercy to all people. He is no respecter of persons.

This is shown in the lives of the Christians at Colosse. The goodness and mercy of God is laid out to a watching world as the Christians live out their lives to the glory of God. Paul is stirring up the grace of God in the hearts of the Christians and where they now stand in relation to God. They are in Christ and have the eternal life in them and the hope of everlasting glory. They are the people of God and of the household of faith and therefore have now dignity and purpose in the family of God. They are the work of God in the frail vessels of human form.

We who believe on Christ have a peculiar dignity, lifted up from the dirt of sins and this tawdry world. We are the possession of Christ and do not need to carp or complain ever again. The riches of God dwell in us and the express revelation of Jesus is our daily view. Let us enter into all that God has purposed for us - outsiders who have been brought into the heavenly experiences of the Christian life, and deep and ultimate blessings of the holy God.

What is our hope of this eternal glory?

It is the person of Christ in us, the marks of the eternal God in our lives that lead us to salvation and holiness of life. There is no other hope for us in this life or the next.

V28 Perfect

"…whom we proclaim, admonishing every man and teaching every man in all wisdom, that we may present every man perfect in Christ Jesus;"

The gospel is proclaimed. It is proclaimed in all its richness and glory before all who will listen. The purpose of God's message is the changing of the dark human view into the glorious light of God; the resurrection of dead souls to eternal life; the beginning again of a new life in Christ. The message is simple and clear… repent and believe. We turn from the sin that infests us and walk in the light of God rather than the light of our own darkened eyes. We believe in the person and work of the only Saviour of souls, the Lord Jesus Christ. He is the centre of the message, for He has humbled Himself and shed His blood that we might be redeemed from the empty way of life we all follow in this life.

When the gospel is spoken, we implore people to turn and be saved. It is the imperative. We must believe or be lost eternally. The choice is very clear and stark. Believe or perish. We teeter on the brink of disaster and hardly know it. We feel so safe and secure until trouble comes along and we are cast into doubt and sorrow. This often drives us to God and the search for a Saviour's love. This is one of the situations that God often uses to bring people to faith, because we will never come to God until we see our abject need.

If we continue on the natural trajectory of our lives, we will land in perdition. This is the message of warning from a loving God. He is holy and all His judgments are just and holy. He warns us of impending judgment for our sin and to seek the refuge in a Saviour's salvation so that we are safe from the consequences of our own folly. The cost to us is free. We are set free from our sin and given new lives to live for the glory of God and the comfort of our souls.

We must be clear about who we are trusting in. There are many false views of Christ and many deniers of His person, who He is as the eternal God, and able to save and change the human heart. We tend to make a Jesus after our own ideas rather than looking intently into the Scripture and finding out what He is like as He presents Himself to us. It is easy to construct an idol, and many do this and are deluded. Jesus is not like us, He identifies with us, but is the perfect God and lived a perfectly obedient life, unlike us. His motivations are different from ours and all His words and deeds were for the glory of the Father in heaven. We must be sure we are really following Him and not someone presented to us falsely.

We follow His perfect ways and become more and more like Him. This is the purpose of our Christian life to refine us and conform us to the view of God and not our own ideas. We need to be taught in all the wisdom of God, and we continue in the Lord, learning and growing all through our Christian lives.

The purpose of the Apostle Paul in this letter is to teach the Christians what Christ is like that they might be more Christ-like in life and speech. One day we will be presented as perfect before the Father as the redeemed and glorified people of God. Until then we seek to be like Him, as He is revealed to us in this letter, and in all the Scripture.

"that I may know him, and the power of his resurrection, and the fellowship of his

sufferings, becoming conformed to his death, if by any means I may attain to the resurrection from the dead. Not that I have already obtained, or am already made perfect; but I press on, that I may take hold of that for which also I was taken hold of by Christ Jesus."

Philippians 3:10-12

V29 Labour

"... for which I also labour, striving according to his working, which works in me mightily."

The Apostle Paul laboured, that the Church of Jesus Christ would be strong and be presented holy and perfect before God. He worked to embed the message of the gospel in the hearts and minds of the Christians, so that they would not be taken from the truth or embrace any kind of error.

Paul is showing us in this letter, the attributes of Jesus Christ so that the believers will not be lead astray and follow a false Christ. To see Christ in all His glory, builds up our faith to trust Him more and follow Him more closely. This is the purpose of this book, that we might see the Lord and the depths of the sacrifice He made for us. This will cause us to be grateful and lift our eyes off our own situation and focus them on Him who we love.

Paul is not doing and saying these things by his own efforts. It is the power of God within him, as the Holy Spirit guides him and directs all that he says and does. How wonderful to know that God is in charge of our life, and we don't have to fret or worry about any situation, no matter how dire it may be. God is able to sustain us. We have the amazing example of the Apostle Paul to show us that way, and the rich spiritual blessings we receive at God's hand. Life was in no way easy for the Apostle, yet it was full of blessing and usefulness. God lifted him out of hatred and bitterness and set him on a rock so that he could serve the Lord in all the ways that he did.

The same is true for us if we are believers and are following Him. It does not matter particularly about our earthly circumstances, for the Lord purposes all things, and we rejoice in His daily provision and blessing. What is important is our dedication and devotion to the Lord, to live every part of our lives for His glory. We keep ourselves in the love of God and self-discipline, to walk worthy steps through each day. The enemy will be kept at bay, as our faith is placed in the only Saviour, our Saviour, Jesus.

Paul is not exclusive in his experience of the mighty working of the Holy Spirit, we also can know the depths of His power as we live from day to day. He will teach us and give us opportunities to serve and witness, as He allows. He loves us, so may we trust His judgment as He leads us through each day. Let us not allow guilt and blame to ruin our souls and any root of bitterness grow up. We are not able, but our God is able…

Colossians Chapter Two

23 verses

Colossians Chapter Two

V1 Struggle

"For I desire to have you know how greatly I struggle for you, and for those at Laodicea, and for as many as have not seen my face in the flesh; "

This verse follows on from the end of the last chapter and extends the sentiment expressed there for the spiritual well-being of the Christians at Colosse and all who would read this letter, including us. Paul seems to realise that his words are not just his words but will last the test of time. He speaks to us still, down through the Millenia and his voice, God's voice, is not dulled. Paul wants them to know his love for them, even though he faces death, that they will listen and obey the voice of the Lord.

Paul has had many struggles and continues to have many struggles because of the ministry that God has called him to do. Paul has suffered beatings, shipwreck, violence, imprisonments, threats, called up before authorities, and personal loss. Paul works to keep himself and takes no funds from any church or organisation. He is dedicated to the development of the spiritual life of the church and is the example, for all time of sacrificial living and serving.

He loves the Christians at Colosse and also Laodicea and also all of us, who he has never seen or known. He loves the body of Christ first and foremost and is seeking to build them up in holy faith and love for the Lord. Paul is building strong Christians so that the church will stand firm in the Lord and hold closely to the Apostle's doctrine and teaching.

His expression is full of emotion. His passion and desire is for the people of God and his own life is forfeit for their sakes. He describes his life as a "struggle" and so it is. He has given up all the comforts and success in this life, to have the prize in the life to come.

"Don't you know that those who run in a race all run, but one receives the prize? Run like that, that you may win. Every man who strives in the games exercises self-control in all things. Now they do it to receive a corruptible crown, but we an incorruptible."

1 Corinthians 9:24-25

This is the pattern for every Christian. We cannot serve God and this world. We choose who we serve and what we give our time to. God will honour our choices for His glory and prosper our work in the Lord.

V2 Assurance

"...that their hearts may be comforted, they being knit together in love, and gaining all riches of the full assurance of understanding, that they may know the mystery of God, both of the Father and of Christ,"

Paul is seeking to comfort the hearts of the people of God, so that they are bound together in love and devotion to each other, as well as the Lord. We cannot get very far without Christian fellowship and the bond of face-to-face filial love that we share for each other. It is very challenging to have to be alone, as the Apostle Paul is finding in his prison situation.

As Christian people we seek and need the understanding about God, who He is and what His purposes are in this world and in the world to come. We need to know the assurance that we belong to Christ and that His word is the centre of our lives and our daily bread. We must know the Father God and also the Lord Jesus Christ, through the Holy Spirit who lives in us.

As we grow in grace and in the maturity of Christian assurance, our knowledge of God and our Saviour, Jesus also grows, and we will understand the Word of God more clearly and deeply. As we walk with the Lord, we rejoice to know Him and that His fellowship is with us in our lives. This is the way of the Christian's assurance. As we grow in Him, our confidence also grows and we make progress in holiness.

V3 Treasures

"...In whom are hidden all the treasures of wisdom and knowledge."

Such a short phrase that summarises so much!

There is such treasure hidden in our Lord Jesus Christ. All the treasures of wisdom and knowledge are bound up in Him, His mind and heart are full of all goodness and the love of God. If we want wisdom, we ask of Him and He will give us His wisdom. If we want knowledge, we ask of Him and He enlightens our mind to know the Scriptures and interpret them aright. The book of the Scripture is the very Word of God and gives us all the knowledge revealed about the holy God. As we read the Scripture and believe we can know Him.

To know Christ is to know the fount of all knowledge and wisdom. What a privilege we possess as believers in that blessed name! We are tuned into the very wisdom that made our world and all the worlds, in fact, everything that exists. He knows the reasons for all things, and though He does not reveal everything to us, we can trust in Him because of who He is and who He has revealed Himself to be. He understands the end of the thing from the beginning though we do not, but we must not, for we live by faith and not by sight. Some knowledge is for God alone, for we are not able to bear it.

"Trust in the LORD with all your heart, and don't lean on your own understanding. In all your ways acknowledge him, and he will make your paths straight."

Proverbs 3:5-6

We must rest on that superior knowledge and trust His eternal judgments that they are right and fair. We do not substitute our frail human sense of justice for His, for we are faulty and do not know all the circumstances. Whatever happens to us, we will trust in Him and rest on that amazing knowledge and that all-wise heart that loves us so much.

The person of our Lord Jesus is precious to us, far above all our vaunted understanding and foolish ways. We worship Him because He is worthy of all we have and are, indeed we stand worthless before Him. Only His mighty love can accept us and change us and make us wise and able to know Him. As we know His person, we are made wise and full of knowledge, but only as we put away the sins that so easily entangle us and put on the righteousness that God gives us. As we draw so close, we become more and more like Him and worship Him more readily and more often. We appreciate His presence above the company of all others and see the astounding treasure that is bound up in His person.

Beloved, all knowledge and wisdom is bound up in Him, so let us follow increasingly closely and throw off everything that hinders us from drawing near...

V4 Delude

"Now this I say that no one may delude you with persuasiveness of speech"

The Apostle Paul is covering all the bases by setting before the believers the Lord Jesus. Only their true view of Him will protect them from false teachers and false doctrine. It is the same for us today.

It is easy to find yourself deluded by fancy preachers and people who exude confidence in themselves and live glamorous lives. Some people seem to have everything, and others have very little. It seems that God helps people who are wily and smart and know how to get what they want, while those who make sacrifices for His sake, are left without.

We keep our focus on Christ, the author and finisher of our faith and the only one who can bring us safely through the minefield, that is this Christian life, and bring us safe to God.

Our minds must be grounded in the Word of God. We must know it for ourselves and not be relying on preachers to tell us what to think and believe. There are so many false prophets, teachers and the like, out there in the public domain that it is frightening. We live in dark days, perhaps the end days, when there will be great delusion and many so-called "believers" falling away from the faith. They fall away because they did not believe on the only Saviour, but just following an idea and a convenience for them.

The media is so endearing. It looks so glamorous and draws us in with sight and sound. We hear the grandiose words and the fake promises that are really just "self-help" strategies and techniques. There is no living faith and no love for Christ at all. There are platitudes and a nodding ascent to some kind of belief in a vague Bible, but nothing living or breathing. There is no Holy Spirit of God in any of it, despite the vaulted efforts to invoke His presence. He is dishonoured in the end and that is a very serious matter.

Caution is the key. Read, study, meditate on the Scripture and guard your mind and heart from all that is evil out there, carried out in the name of Christianity.

"Beloved, don't believe every spirit, but test the spirits, whether they are of God,

because many false prophets have gone out into the world."

1 John 4:1

Paul is ensuring that the believers and all the church of God are in no doubt about sound doctrine and have a clear view of the person of Christ. Be persuaded of all the right things and shun every evil word.

V5 Steadfastness

"For though I am absent in the flesh, yet am I with you in the spirit, rejoicing and seeing your order, and the steadfastness of your faith in Christ."

How wonderful to be steadfast in Christ the Lord...

This is the ideal state to be in as we walk with the Lord. To walk with Him steadily and strongly every day without wavering and not falling back, no losing our footing and stumbling around - no falling into sin and succumbing to temptations. To walk worthily with the Lord and please Him every day is our goal. We are not yet made perfect, but we are steadfast.

"...the testing of your faith produces endurance. Let endurance have its perfect work, that you may be perfect and complete, lacking in nothing."

James 1:3-4

It is possible to live a godly life in this world and to please the Lord in all we say and do. It involves the testing of our faith, and that severely, as James points out in his book. But the striving to overcome and the battles against the flesh, the world and the devil, only serve to make us complete.

Paul the Apostle sees these qualities in the Christians at Colosse and identifies with them in the Spirit. He cannot be with them in the body, as he is in prison, but his soul goes out to them, in love and fellowship, and hence the letter. Paul rejoices with them as they rejoice in Christ.

"Don't be grieved; for the joy of The LORD is your strength."

Nehemiah 8:10

This is what sets the Christians apart from the one who does not believe. We should be the happiest people on earth, as we are children in the family of God, have a royal inheritance with the saints of God, and know Christ as our loving and constant companion. There is no fretting or worry or wrong motivations in this state of living. All is peace with God, and nothing harms us or disturbs our rest. Life is orderly and settled and full of hope and faithful acts of grace and mercy. We rejoice in the Lord always.

All this is bound up with the closeness of our relationship with our Saviour. Our deep sense of gratitude to Him and the devotion of love is ever on our minds and hearts and lips. We love Him because He loved us first and gave Himself for us. We keep our repentance to the forefront of our thinking and have short accounts with the Lord. We go wrong and put it right straight away. Therefore, we are joyful and free people, free to be righteous and kind. Though we may be separated from other believers, we are joined in heart and soul and can commune together in the bond of peace in the Spirit. We encourage each other in the Lord and wait for the great day when Christ will be revealed, and our steadfastness will give way to eternal perfection.

V6 Walk

"As therefore you received Christ Jesus, the Lord, walk in him,"

We receive Christ by faith, so the rest of our lives from that point are walked and lived in faith in God.

We walk worthy of the calling by which He has called us heavenward. We do not fall back on depending on ourselves or the people around us but take the responsibility for our spiritual lives and build ourselves up in our holy faith. Our love is not for this world, but for Christ and His word. Our hope is in the sure promises of God and not in the empty words of other people.

As we have been forgiven, so we forgive and find ourselves praying for unlikely people, those who oppose us and even hurt us. The change in our mindset could not be greater, as we fix our will at the bottom of our priorities and put God's will at the top. The subjugation of self is the greatest challenge, and without the saving faith we receive from God, we cannot succeed.

We start our Christian lives with the power of God, and we continue in that power. We do nothing that would grieve the Holy Spirit into silence in our lives but continue in the living of life in a righteous way.

We begin as cleansed and forgiven people, and we continue in that same way. It is the way to life and peace and a deep inner happiness that no one can take away. We give up all for Christ and receive all that we could desire in Him alone.

"Forgetting the things which are behind, and stretching forward to the things which are before, I press on toward the goal for the prize of the high calling of God in Christ Jesus."

Philippians 3:13-14

We press on, not resting on our accomplishments and not drowning in our sins but walking steadily on with our Saviour and Lord.

V7 Established

"… rooted and built up in him, and established in the faith, even as you were taught, abounding in it in thanksgiving."

If we are not rooted in Christ, we will not be built up in Him. There must be repentance before there is sanctification. This does not only apply to the beginning of the Christian life at conversion, but is true and a feature all the way through our lives. We cannot be established in our faith if there is no initial grounding. We need good teaching and good teachers today more than ever because the times are evil. Yet they are few and far between. There is extraordinary falsehood everywhere, and extraordinary claims taken to men who vaunt themselves on the media. But it is so very difficult to find sound, godly Christian fellowship in our local lives. The church of Jesus Christ has been decimated by error and self-promotion. We have become trivial and shallow and wrong.

What are we to do?

We must go back to the beginning and relearn the deep doctrines of the Scripture and remember what we were once taught. Perhaps we were never taught it, and have endured all kinds of false preaching and teaching. We need to revisit the Word of God and find out what God says to us and what His character is like and what He requires of us. This is quite different from the easy sound bite that seems to please too many of us.

To revisit our testimony is a good start and to find out if we are really of the faith of the Scripture and what we really believe. It is imperative that we are trusting in the right Jesus and not our own imagination. Then we must build up our faith as we study the Word of God and put it into practice in our lives. We repent of our waywardness and stick closely to the truth revealed.

If we are established in the faith, taught and keeping to the Word of God, it will cause us to abound in thanksgiving and make us grateful for all the Lord has done for us. We will cease complaining about our circumstances and be glad for the daily blessings we receive. The striving for the things of this life will stop and therefore we will become deeper and stronger in faith and love.

The basis of it all is Christ. Many have forgotten Him and put him far down the list of priorities in their lives, and some are thinking that they follow Him but it is not the Christ of the Bible. Some are part time and put on the robes of righteousness on Sunday for the church service and then revert to their own clothes the rest of the time. Some are glad to know Him and tell others about what the Lord has done for them. Others do not have a testimony at all, but are relying on their works to be better than others and that they will be allowed into the kingdom on that basis.

Only Christ is the bedrock, so let us throw off the hindrances and focus on eternity and the life that is to come. If we feather our nests in the now, we will have no love for Christ, no inheritance in the next life and no thanksgiving to the Lord.

Paul is addressing these issues and building the spiritual knowledge of the saints, so that they will be faithful believers and love the Lord and what He has done for them. Let us also build and get established in the faith and foster the mindset of thanksgiving, and we will be deeply rooted in our faith and stand in the time of testing.

V8 Tradition

"Be careful that you don't let anyone rob you through his philosophy and vain deceit, after the tradition of men, after the elements of the world, and not after Christ."

Paul is directly addressing the fundamental issues we face today in all our church situations. We cannot sustain our powers of judgement and ignore what is going on around us. Paul says if we do, we will be robbed of our faith and devotion to the Lord Jesus and lose the cutting edge of our love for Him and other people around us. Philosophy abounds and everyone has their own ideas, walking in the light of their own understanding, but not seeking the wisdom of God. The gospel that will bring people to faith is not preached and people accept the self-help advice and think God is helping them.

It is all vanity and vexation of purpose. It deceives people and builds the speaker and the hearer up in the pride of their own thinking. These man-made and man-propagated philosophies will drag us down and lead us astray. They are entirely this-world orientated and do not teach the way to God. They are sinful and will lead us away from the Lord and teach us to rely on fables, which will ultimately let us down when the going gets difficult.

Science has been infiltrated with materialistic philosophy and has led to the blinding of the human mind to the glory for the created order. Science has been hijacked by this materialism and it has infiltrated our culture to a detrimental degree. People are living like there is no God, because we have swallowed the falsehood in the name of Science. Science is now the new religion and has set itself up against the Creator to its own detriment. Scientific findings are interpreted by the philosophical mindset of the enquirer, and we see the godless belief systems being foisted on our society and taught to our children. We follow the tradition of men and not the revealed Word of the Lord. We close our minds and hearts to Him and prefer our own way. People set themselves up against the Lord and many follow them, because they are accepted as "scientists" or "clever." This so not what the Bible teaches, and we are now seeing the unravelling of the mindset of the atheistic world view and true science is showing us something quite different.

The Scripture is true and God's way is the way to life and peace. Our own way leads us to death and the destruction of our minds and hearts. Our minds become dim and we are deluded and our hearts atrophy and we do not accept God anymore. God tells us plainly what He thinks of the worldly mindset. He says it is foolish and will destroy our eternity. People do not believe God or pay attention to His reasoning and His verdict on our lives, and so find themselves treading the path away from God and into unbelief and spiritual death. Paul does not want this for His Christian brothers and sisters, and so he is writing this letter and showing the glory of the Lord Jesus. Only as we see Him, will we be kept from error and all falsehood.

"Every Scripture is God-breathed and profitable for teaching, for reproof, for correction, and for instruction in righteousness,"

2 Timothy 3:16

V9 Godhead

"For in him all the fullness of the Godhead dwells bodily,"

Here we have the certainty that the Lord Jesus Christ is the second person of the trinity of God. He is not just the man Christ Jesus, but all the fullness of God dwells in Him, in His character and physical being. In His body He is no less God than before the incarnation and Jesus lost nothing of His authority, power and glory, by taking on a human body. The Lord Jesus Christ is the very God, the maker of the ends of the earth and the Redeemer of human souls. He has the right and power to forgive sin, for He has paid its terrible price on the cross. He is the Saviour of the world and the Judge of all the earth.

Within the confines of the physical body of Christ lives the full power of the Holy Spirit and the divine nature and power of the Son of God. In becoming a man, He in no way set aside any of His divine attributes but veiled His glory that He might live among us and die to be our Saviour and Lord. We see a glimpse of that glory at the Transfiguration, where the glory of the Lord shone out from Him and was revealed to the few disciples who were there at that time. We see the pure love of the suffering Saviour as He hung on the cross and laid down His life for His own. We see His power set forth in the resurrection, when the Lord of Life raised Himself as the eternal God and glorious Son of the Father. He is the conqueror of death and hell, and no one can stand in His presence without righteousness.

God is found wholly in Christ. The person who does not seek Christ does not seek God. The one who is not satisfied with Christ, desires something more than God! We convey our foolishness in rejecting the Lord Jesus, for there is no one above Him and no one else like Him.

If we possess Christ, we have the Father also. If Christ is in us, then we are indwelt by the eternal God and are redeemed and chosen beings who reflect His glory and are made to be like Him.

"Whoever denies the Son, the same doesn't have the Father. He who confesses the Son has the Father also."

1 John 2:23

V10 Complete

"And you have been made complete in Christ, who is the head over every ruler and authority."

Without Christ we are dead in sin and insensible to spiritual life and blessing. Without Christ we cannot know God nor understand anything about Him or know Him personally. But in Christ we are made complete in every way. Our souls are alive to God, and we are truly alive! We can choose the right and reject the wrong and live with a clear and pure conscience before God and other people.

The work of Christ on the cross of Calvary in paying the penalty for our sin, is enough to satisfy the demands for recompense, of the law of God. The fallenness of our being is made up through what He has done for us. It is personal and Jesus deals in great love with each one of His people. To know Christ in our life and to be personally loved by Him, is the fulfilment of all that we are as human beings. We need look for, or toward, no other, but only to Christ.

When we are right with God, we are really right, and all our fretting goes to the cross and not to ourselves. We can cast our burdens on the Lord, and He will sustain us. It is the remedy for all of life's trials and troubles and the answer to all the problems that we face. It is hard to trust people, because they are not able to sustain us, but the person of Christ is able to save us and keep us right through to the end of our life. He is utterly trustworthy and loves us despite knowing all the rotten things about us that others don't !

He is the majesty on high. No one is above Him or can challenge Him in any way. Every ruler and authority in heaven and on earth is under His jurisdiction and control. He is the sovereign ruler over all the world leaders and judges and authorities that we are all subject to. He decides the beginning and the end of our trials and our blessings and works all things out to conform to His holy will. God's people are at the centre of His heart, and they are the apple of His eye... No one can touch them without His permission, as we know from the story of Job. Satan himself has no power over the believer and cannot hurt us or offend us, but only annoy. The weakest saint of God has the victory over this mighty foe, for he is beaten already. We pray to be delivered from his temptations that we might escape all evil and live triumphant lives through Christ.

This is our complete salvation, and we will enter into the full assurance of it and the full immortality of body, mind and soul, when the Lord will return for us. Beloved, we have a glorious inheritance in a life with Christ now, and in the kingdom to come. Indeed, it is already here, and we recognise our position in it and rejoice.

"For our citizenship is in heaven, from where we also wait for a Saviour, the Lord Jesus Christ; who will change the body of our humiliation to be conformed to the body of his glory, according to the working by which he is able even to subject all things to himself."

Philippians 3:20-21

The Lord Jesus is able to change us in profound ways and conform our thinking and doing to be like Him. Even in this world we experience His power in our lives to change and grow our spiritual life and draw us near to His presence daily. In the end He will have all the pre-eminence and will change us into glorious beings, like Himself. This is the prospect for every saint of God who believes in Christ and is walking with Him.

V11 Separate

"..in whom you were also circumcised with a circumcision not made with hands, in the putting off of the body of the sins of the flesh, in the circumcision of Christ;"

Circumcision was a big issue for the Jewish believers, but in this verse, we see another circumcision, the circumcision of the soul. The outward show is as nothing and only feeds the religious feelings and exclusivity of the Jewish religion. It was superseded by the institution of the early Church and passed into the history of the Jewish religion and practice. To carry on the practice after the coming of Christ in the incarnation is to deny Christ. To mix the old and the new is the essence of the teaching of the false teachers in Paul's day who were called the concision and are cut off from Christ. To carry on with the figure of the outward sign is to deny the inner work of the Spirit and the work that was accomplished on the cross.

God requires more that the outward signs of religion and therefore separates His people to holiness of life in the Spirit. The inner workings of the circumcision of the

Holy Spirit is the separation from the world that God is looking for in the lives of His people. This does not involve any outward ritual but the sanctifying work of the Spirit to bring the believer into close fellowship with the Father and the Son.

No human being can administer this spiritual ritual, but only the Holy Spirit within the life of the Christian believer. It is a spiritual work and not any outward, fleshly manifestation. Those days of the old law and the old covenant are over and now the new has come in Christ. It is a better and permanent covenant that cannot fail, for it is with God, between the three persons of the godhead, to save a fallen group of people. The covenant was ratified at the cross of Calvary and shown in power and glory in the resurrection. This is the basis for the new covenant, not on outward show, but the glory of the life of God within a person.

The entrance into the kingdom of God is not through outward works of religion or good works in the world, but the setting apart of the life for God. It is the expression of the life of faith, a life that trusts God completely and will obey the Word of the Scripture and put selfish consideration away. The inner circumcision will result in a life that is separate from this world and rejecting of the unfruitful works of darkness that abound in our day and embrace the life of holiness and obedience. It is the cutting off of the signs of the flesh that abound in us still, and the putting to death the immoral deeds of the body.

Christ took on Himself the form of a servant and was obedient to the Father, even to the death on the cross! How much more we should rejoice to obey the Lord and walk in the way of His commandments. We separate ourselves from sin and self and live our lives in increasing fellowship and love for the Lord Jesus Christ. This is true circumcision-circumcision of the heart and mind.

V12 Baptism

"having been buried with him in baptism, in which you were also raised with him through faith in the working of God, who raised him from the dead."

Baptism does not save us or do any spiritual good for the salvation of our souls. It is not a precursor for salvation, nor does it set us apart for salvation. Many are baptised and die in their sins, having never come to personal repentance in Christ. It is a cogent and personal act of choice for someone who has trusted in Christ and wants to follow the example of Christ and be immersed in the waters of baptism. It is a sign of something spiritual that has happened in their lives and an outward confession of faith in Christ the Saviour.

The witness of baptism shows the reality of what has happened in the soul of the person being baptised. The person goes down into the water of baptism and is buried in it to show the going down into death of the Lord Jesus as He paid the price of the sins of His people. The person is then bodily raised out of the water to signify the raising of Christ from the dead as the victorious Saviour and Lord of all. The Christian is given new life to serve God and glorify Him forever. We identify with the death and resurrection of the Lord Jesus for we have died to sin and are resurrected to a new life in Christ through our faith in the power of God that raised Jesus from then dead.

"You were buried therefore with him through baptism to death, that just like Christ was raised from the dead through the glory of the Father, so we also might walk in newness of life."

Romans 6:4

The spectacle of baptism is an outward witness of the inner work of the Spirit of God in salvation. We are raised to a new life in Christ to walk in the power of the Spirit in obedience and faith.

"This is a symbol of baptism, which now saves you—not the putting away of the filth of the flesh, but the answer of a good conscience toward God, through the resurrection of Jesus Christ,"

1 Peter 3:21

This verse follows on in the Scripture, from the picture given of the salvation of Noah and his family in the ark through the waters of the flood. They were rescued by the Lord from the destruction and judgment of the pre-diluvian world and brought to new life through the salvation of God. So also, the picture of baptism shows the salvation of God in the life of the believer and is therefore the salvation of baptism. The baptism shows what we have been saved from and saved to.

It is not the washing of the flesh but the confession of the work of conscience in the soul that has brought the person to repentance and faith. There is no salvation without repentance and faith and therefore no baptism either. We are brought into a new and glorious life as Jesus was raised from the dead and bought eternal life for us.

"Philip opened his mouth, and beginning from this Scripture, preached to him Jesus. As they went on the way, they came to some water, and the eunuch said, "Behold, here is water. What is keeping me from being baptised?" He commanded the chariot to stand still, and they both went down into the water, both Philip and

*the eunuch, and he baptised him. When
they came up out of the water, the Spirit
of the Lord caught Philip away, and the
eunuch didn't see him any more, for he
went on his way rejoicing."*

Acts 8:35-39

The Ethiopian is constrained to be
baptised after confession of Christ and he
and Philip go down into the water and the
Ethiopian is baptised. There is rejoicing for
the newly converted Ethiopian who has
obeyed the Lord. So also, for the Christian
believer who has trusted in Christ and
wishes to identify themselves with their
Lord and Saviour. It is an outward and
abiding witness of an inner and living
spiritual event that has happened to them
and a reality that they now live in. We are
now dead to this world and made alive in
Christ for the salvation of our souls.

Baptism in the New Testament is never a
precursor to salvation. The faith in Christ
and the confession of personal change in
the Believer comes first and the desires to
identify with the Lord by going down into
His death and being raised in resurrection
power is the outworking of the personal
faith. Paul is reminding the Christians at
Colosse about their faith and obedience to

the Lord in baptism and is constraining them to continue in that way. So as the Christian looks back at the event of their baptism, they are encouraged to keep following the Lord and obeying Him.

V13 Forgiven

"You were dead through your trespasses and the uncircumcision of your flesh. He made you alive together with him, having forgiven us all our trespasses,"

Here in this verse, we have the reason why God had to choose us first in order to save us and make us spiritually alive. Without the Lord we have no faith, no love and no hope. We are dead in our trespasses because of our sin and the sins that we commit daily. This sin separates us from the Lord and makes us insensible to His voice and His pleading. Only when the Holy Spirit works in our lives do we start to feel the destitute nature of our state and we begin to seek God.

In our fleshly lives we are uncircumcised. We live our earthly lives lost to the Lord, with no love for Him or desire to know Him personally. As we have discussed in verse eleven, the circumcision that God requires is the circumcision of heart that binds us to God and takes us away from the things of this vain world. We would never choose God, left to our own devices, but we will cling on to the sin that so easily besets us, unless we are shown the seriousness of the consequences of it, and the cost to our eternal souls, if we neglect this great salvation. The consequences of rejecting the provision of God are so serious and everlasting, that we must consider the end of our choices and where we will spend the ages of eternity. We must be forgiven, for to face the holy God with no salvation is serious in the extreme.

However, those who do come to God, are made spiritually alive in Christ and have the power of God residing in them, to give them desires after holiness and the humility to follow the Lord Jesus wherever He might lead them. God gives the ability to choose him, when our inner eyes are opened to see the truth about ourselves and the truth of the gospels message. He sets us free to make a good choice and not a wretched one. To be alive in Christ, and to Christ, is the greatest state to be in. To know His love in our lives and to be able to conquer the giants of doubt and temptation that infiltrate our thinking and doing, is the power of God.

How wonderful to know for sure that your sins are all forgiven, and you are regarded by God as a holy person, because of the Lord Jesus. We are forgiven because of Him and we continue to thrive in our Christian lives because of Him.

We fight the uncircumcised desires and practices of the flesh and put to death the desires of the physical life in this world that incline our hearts and minds away from Christ. Our redeemed self puts on righteousness and seeks the spiritual life found only through faith in Jesus. Anything else is worldly and unprofitable for it will not stand the test of God at the end of our lives. Many will find their work and witness for God as *"wood, hay and stubble"* which will be burnt in the fires of testing. There will be no works of righteousness to give to the Lord, for they are so contaminated by our flesh, that they will not survive.

Beloved, we rejoice to know our sins are forgiven and cast into the sea of God's forgetfulness, and we deny self and the flesh to put on righteousness and produce work fitting for the Lord. Then our hearts will be truly circumcised to God and acceptable to Him. Then we will be alive together with Christ.

"He will again have compassion on us. He will tread our iniquities under foot; and you will cast all their sins into the depths of the sea."

Micah 7:19

V14 Nailed

"…wiping out the handwriting in ordinances which was against us; and he has taken it out of the way, nailing it to the cross;"

Here is the central kernel of the blessing in Christ. The record of all our sin is wiped out because all our sin is nailed to the cross of Christ, and has been paid for by Him. The permanent, written handwriting of accusation and blame is expunged, and our sins are remembered no more.

It has all been taken out of the way and paid for on the cross. The picture is strong and specific. It is nailed to the cross never to get down and bother us again. The record of our sin is taken out of our record and it has really been dealt with and we will never be accused of any of it. This fact should bring us great joy and great relief. The law has no more hold on the Christian and there is no more condemnation for the believer.

The handwriting upheld by the ordinances of the Old Testament is now gone and we are not required to do any of it and are therefore free people. The grace we experience in Christ sets us free to live and there is no remembrance made of our sin any more. We are not subject to the shadows of the spiritual life in the physical kingdom, for the kingdom has now come and the old has passed away.

"There is therefore now no condemnation to those who are in Christ Jesus, who don't walk according to the flesh, but according to the Spirit."

Romans 8:1

All the blame has been put away with the nailing of the handwriting of the dead ordinances on the cross of Christ. God is now for us, not against us, as we are covered by the sacrifice of the Lord Jesus and are now free people. The ceremonies have gone and with them the admission of guilt and blame. Christ has done way with the ceremonies, with no memory of the obligation to God we carry around in our souls because of our sin. It is all forgiven...

"You will know the truth, and the truth will make you free....If therefore the Son makes you free, you will be free indeed."
John 8:32 and 36

It is the truth in Christ and the truth that is Christ, that sets us free and not the observing of dead ordinances that are against the grace of God.

V15 Triumphing

"...having stripped the principalities and the powers, he made a show of them openly, triumphing over them in it."

The triumph of the cross cannot be held high enough for it to be shown for what it is. What was accomplished there we will never really be able to grasp. The enormity of the victory that was achieved for us and the depths and breadths of the payment for our sin will never be realised by any human. The Lord Jesus has gained the victory over every enemy of our soul, and it is so extreme, He is able to save completely anyone who comes to Him. The victory is so universal that He is able to put to flight every power that raises itself up against Him or His precious people.

"He is the head of the body, the assembly, who is the beginning, the firstborn from the dead; that in all things he might have the pre-eminence."

Colossians 1:18

This verse we are studying says that He showed the evil powers and authorities up for what they really are. He showed the wickedness in the hearts of the human authorities by the way they treated Him at His death. The record we have in the Scripture is the sight of despicable human beings full of envy and wrath, spewing out their hatred on the Son of God. He dealt with them with such dignity and majesty that they could not understand.

The treachery of one of His own disciples fills us with fear, lest we should also be found in such a state. The story of Judas is a sorry tale of the cowardice and greed in the human heart. The powers of darkness gathered around the Saviour of the world and tried their utmost spite against Him, knowing they could never succeed yet hounding Him to the cross. The dignity and divine majesty of the Lord Jesus is clearly seen in all He said and did and shows us that He really is who He says He is.

Jesus put to death the power of Satan, so he can conquer the people of God no longer. The victory is complete, because the price is paid and all spite and sorrow is gone forever for all who will believe. Satan is finally shown to be who he really is and is stripped of all his vaunted pomp and show. He is low and beaten and cannot hurt us anymore.

Christ is the conquering king, as the sign that was put above the cross tells us.

JESUS OF NAZARETH, THE KING OF THE JEWS.

His triumph is complete because He has bought a people for Himself who are now delivered from the wrath to come and who will serve Him and reign with Him in all eternity.

"I saw the heaven opened, and behold, a white horse, and he who sat on it is called Faithful and True. In righteousness he judges and makes war. His eyes are a flame of fire, and on his head are many crowns. He has names written and a name written which no one knows but he himself. He is clothed in a garment sprinkled with blood. His name is called "The Word of God." The armies which are in heaven followed him on white horses, clothed in white, pure, fine linen.Out of his mouth proceeds a sharp, double-edged sword, that with it he should strike the nations. He will rule them with an iron rod.He treads the wine press of the

fierceness of the wrath of God, the Almighty.He has on his garment and on his thigh a name written,
"KING OF KINGS, AND LORD OF LORDS."

Revelation 19:11-16

V16 Judging

"Let no one therefore judge you in eating, or in drinking, or with respect to a feast day or a new moon or a Sabbath day,"

Since the ceremonial and everything outside the moral law is now passed away, we do not hold to the keeping of traditional religious feasts and days of religious observance. Indeed, the rules for the culture of living have passed away and we are free to choose many things that we do and pay attention to.

We are not to judge each other outside the moral law and make value judgments about each other based on what we do in the living of our lives, or even what religious observances we hold to. We are not to judge eating or drinking, what people like to eat, how they eat it, when the eat it, etc... same with drinking. We all make our choices about these issues, and we are set free by the Scripture to do so. We are not to judge about days that are set aside for God, what they are or when they are.

Unfortunately for us we can be legalistic in our outlook and use all kinds of personal prejudicial judgments to oppress other people. This should not be so among Christian people. People love to tell each other what to do and how to do it, and we display the root of pride that is still in our psyche and that feeds that judgment. It is especially prominent in holiday times, as different cultural groups celebrate differently and have various preferences and traditional habits that the Scripture allows. Too many seek to over-ride the Word of God and substitute their own pet likes and dislikes for the various habits of other people. Consequently, divisions arise in the mind, and prejudice grows.

Prejudice is a despicable state of mind and harbours ill will towards people who are different and who have different habits from ourselves. It is the root of all the -isms, the barriers that have grown up between the differing cultural groups, genders, age groups, and so on. We impose our own foolish consciences on other people and make shackles for the feet of the redeemed! This should not be so and is not the way of Christ or Christian people. I am reminded that this is for issues outside the moral law, it is not a free-for-all to do whatever we like. We must not deliberately provoke people either, or make problems where problems do not exist!

Where prejudice shows itself, we must address it, before it spreads and is accepted into the general psyche of the group. Prejudice against anyone is ugly and we should watch our own thought processes and speaking. We should be careful about our language and examine the things we say to make sure they reflect good attitudes and not expressions of prejudicial thinking.

Holidays and special days of celebration are free times and are to be celebrated as we choose. We are free people and must not be put under the yoke of bondage again, as in the group that insisted on circumcision and caused division in the early church. This issue is a continuation of the thought process that sets the Christians free to live their lives for God and not tradition. The old has passed away and the new has come.

V17 Shadow

".... Which are a shadow of the things to come; but the body is Christ's."

The Old Testament ceremonial law, the feasts and the feast days, were the semblances of those that were to come in the eternal kingdom when Christ would come into the world and the gospel message would be openly preached. They are only as it were, symbols of the coming days of glory for the Christian believer. They are shadows of the coming glory in the gospel age and were meant to lift the heart and mind to God in celebration and enjoyment of what God has provided in the reality of the coming Saviour.

They are mere shadows of the reality of the manifestation of Christ and since Christ is now come and made plain to us, there is no more need of them. We do not cling to a phantom when the real person is with us. The Lord has provided good things for us, in our souls and we rejoice in that provision.

"Then he said to them, "Go your way. Eat the fat, drink the sweet, and send portions to him for whom nothing is prepared; for

this day is holy to our Lord. Don't be grieved; for the joy of the LORD is your strength."

Nehemiah 8:10

We enter into the enjoyment in Christ and the provision for our souls in the gospel. The Lord provided for His people abundantly and was not stingy nor did He hold them back from the enjoyment of the fruits of their labours. The Old Testament feasts were celebrations of the mercy and provision of the Lord, both in this world and the coming kingdom. They were all images of the coming kingdom, where all is prepared for the people of God. God provides for our souls in the person of Jesus and in the inner working of the Holy Spirit in our souls. He blesses us with all spiritual blessings in Christ.

God loves His people and will lavish all good things on them, for the good of their spiritual life. God's people are more important to Him than any other consideration in this world. Christ loves the body, the whole group of Christians that have been given to Him as His own inheritance, and He will bring each one safely to the heavenly home. We are His handiwork and are beyond price, for the price paid for us was beyond compare. He will not let His children be torn apart by petty cultural differences that divide and separate. The body of Christ is one unit and is held together by the work of the Holy Spirit in each person as individuals. We will be presented as glorious beings before the throne of God and be with Christ, our head for ever, His glorious church.

All things are given for our enjoyment and good pleasure. Even in the suffering of this present world we are blessed to know that all is working for the good of each one of us. Every Christian can testify to the faithfulness of the Father in the middle of deep troubles. He spreads a table to joy in the life of every one of His children and no one can take the joy of the Christian away from them.

Jesus the Bridegroom will protect His bride, the people of God, and bring her safely into the heavenly kingdom for that great marriage supper. We will there enjoy all good things prepared for us and rejoice to be a part of the feast, for all those around the table will be redeemed people, and all judgment will be over. The reality of the shadows will have come to full fruition and the full light of heaven's day will shine.

"My beloved is mine and I am his; he pastures his flock among the lilies. Before the day breaks and shadows flee..."

Song of Songs 2:16-17

The shadows have now gone, and the full light of gospel revelation is shining. Christ is the embodiment of all these ceremonies and is the manifestation of all the grace and love of God. The light is now shining for all those who will believe. Christ is the fulfilment of these pictures from the Old Testament and is the revelation of them to us. The Apostle is adamant that the old shadows will not linger when the light of day now shines.

Beloved, we rejoice in the Lord Jesus and enter into the reality of knowing Him and experiencing the provision He has made for our souls.

V18 Fleshly

"Let no one rob you of your prize by a voluntary humility and worshipping of the angels, dwelling in the things which he has not seen, vainly puffed up by his fleshly mind,"

It is too easy to be side-tracked by spiritual folly. It is too easy to lose your reward by falling into sins and falling way from the Lord. There are people who seem very spiritual and seem to know a lot about the Scripture and are good at putting their ideas across, especially in the media. They have winning personalities that can draw us to what they say.

Unfortunately, what they say is not wholly right and true and their words are contaminated by error. This error involves a kind of self-righteous, self-conscious humility that is not true but appears to be sincere. Maybe they mean well, maybe they know what they are about, but whatever their motivation it draws people away for the truth of the scripture and to put faith in angels, signs and wonders and all kinds of false doctrines.

Some of the speakers in the media are very full of themselves and focus on the things that they know rather that the study of the Word of God. They talk lucidly and knowledgeable about any number of things that they have worked out in their own lives and have gained a kind of wisdom that is endearing and somewhat helpful to the hearers. But the power of the Word of God is not there, and the doctrine is shallow and applied in a worldly way to the situations that people find themselves in. Speakers can become puffed up very easily, especially if they get some kind of success at what they do and are recognised as important and insightful. Many are a great stumbling block because the Scripture is not presented fully or deeply, and people are just encouraged to self-help their lives into a better place. Prayer becomes a means to an end of getting the things that you want.

The gospel of good news and hope of how a holy God can reconcile sinful people to Himself, gets lost and we get a second-rate message about having God's help in our lives. The rescue message of the cross of Christ is lost in the cacophony of self-promotion. We get tired of the Word and prefer the soundbite of the tele-evangelists and so sound doctrine and the sincere meat of the Word gets left out for psychological insights.

We should shun those who soft-peddle the Word of God and who's words will make us shallow Christians and too worried about the things of this present life and not about the eternal life we possess. We cannot lose our salvation, but we can lose the reward. We can become lazy and complacent about our Christian service and our witness for Christ before the people we know. We can find ourselves dependant on the injection of the preachers who flatter and cajole us, and we become weaker in faith.

We are instructed to resist those who would glorify angels and any being other than Christ. He is our Lord and God, and we worship Him alone. But there are those who are too interested in other heavenly beings and would encourage us to superstition and false worship. The messengers of God in the Revelation of John urged the Apostle to not worship them, because they were created beings just like him.

"I, John, am the one who heard and saw these things. And when I had heard and seen them, I fell down to worship at the feet of the angel who had been showing them to me. But he said to me, "Don't do that! I am a fellow servant with you and with your fellow prophets and with all who keep the words of this scroll. Worship God!"

Revelation 22:8-9

God alone is the uncreated light, and He alone should receive our worship. There are also those who teach that we need the intercession of Mary, angels and worthy Saints to gain favour with God. This is falsehood since the dead have no part with us and Christ alone is the mediator between God and people.

These people look rashly into subjects that they know nothing about, nor is it revealed in the Scripture. They make up false dogma about such entities and confuse many. We accept the headship of Christ and no one else and trust in Him alone for the salvation and sanctification of our souls. Only He through the message of the Word of God can purify us and make us fit for Him. Let us not be puffed up in pride at our own "research" and our own fleshly outlook on the things that are for God. We hold fast to the Apostles doctrine and keep our eyes fixed on Jesus as our Lord and God.

V19 Growth

"... and not holding firmly to the Head, from whom all the body, being supplied and knit together through the joints and ligaments, grows with God's growth."

These falsely humble and superstitious teachers and their followers do not hold to Christ and easily slip away into fleshly and ungodly living. Because they do not hold firmly to Christ and His Word, they fall away, showing themselves not to be of the body of Christ. Christians must hold to Christ, or we will fail and fall...

This body of Christ is so precious, for it is the whole church of God, the full remnant of the people of God who are kept faithful and true by the power of their living and glorious Head – Jesus Christ the righteous one. It is knit together by His power alone and all the parts of it grow to God. Christ supplies the strength to the joints and ligaments that hold the whole body together and facilitate the movement to grow in grace and knowledge of the Word of God. Every part is crucial, for if one part fails, it affects all the others. We are not an unable body, but living stones being built as a strong body of the Lord. As we depend on each other, so we encourage each other in all truth and godliness.

The body of Christ is knit together in the fellowship of the sharing of the holy Scripture and in suffering. Every Christian suffers and the power of encouragement is mighty in the Lord. There is no lording it over one another, but heartfelt humility as we experience hardship and serve the Lord our God with full hearts.

Our growth will be exponential in the body of Christ if we follow the lead of our head. The closer the Christian walks with God, the greater the inner spiritual growth. The more time we spend with God in His Word, the wiser we will be and the more strength we will have. The growth is from the Lord and not a worldly knowledge. It comes from the Word of God and not impressions we might have about our circumstances. The healthy Christian walk with God, sticks close to the commands of God and exercises the disciple of obedience and self-denial. This is not popular with our fallen human psyche but is the pathway to life and peace. It is the only way for the body of Christ to survive, as we need the constant spiritual nourishment from the Lord that we will not fall to pieces and the body fail, just like the human body would do.

If our flesh gets puffed up in self-importance and pride we will fall. We will lose our grip on Christ our head and Master of our souls, and we will stray into all kinds of wayward roads. This will affect us personally and also the whole body of Christ. There is much lack of devotion in our hearts, so we watch ourselves and tutor ourselves with the wisdom of the Spirit to stay close to our Lord and Saviour.

V20 Elements

"If you died with Christ from the elements of the world, why, as though living in the world, do you subject yourselves to ordinances,"

The reasoning here in this verse is clear. If we are part of the spiritual body of Christ and are set apart from the elements that features in this world, why would we insist on continuing on with the outward, fleshly ceremonies that are now defunct. They are unnecessary, as the Lord Jesus has come and is revealed to His people, who follow Him with redeemed hearts and minds and are alive in their souls. The elements and essential components of this vain world are not the motivation of the Christian any more. Our inner eye has been changed and we see and desire the spiritual portion of God. Our hearts are now set after God and His will, and our minds are being conformed to the mind of Christ.

When a person comes to faith in Christ, they die to the things of this life. Their soul has come alive to God and their desires change from being in thrall to this world, to loving the Lord God with all their heart and mind and strength. They cease from chasing the preoccupations of this life and start to live a new life in God. It changes all the priorities from the physical to the spiritual.

The ceremonies and ordinances of the Old Testament era were given to point to the living Saviour that would come to call out His people to respond in repentance and faith in Him. They were pictures and types of the real Lord and not a means in themselves. The believing Israelites would realise this and trust in God in faith just as we do now. They looked forward to the coming Messiah who would release them from the sin and death under which they lived and set them free to serve God as He would command. So, we also look to the Messiah who has come and has saved us from sin and given us faith to believe.

It is illogical to look back to days of shadow, when the Lord has already come, and all the prophecies have been fulfilled and all the pictures have become reality. We serve the living Lord Jesus and have the revelation of His person in the Scripture, so why would we go backwards to the replaced pictures? The Christian is dead to the elements of this life and lives

for another life in Christ, alive in soul to
spiritual elements and God-orientated
living. The Apostle seems incredulous that
a Christian would seek to return to
shadows rather than enter into the light of
the gospel reality. We put off the now out-
of-date ways and put on the new and
living way of life in Jesus Christ the only
Saviour. Anything else is just worldly
mindedness.

V21 Don't

"Don't handle, nor taste, nor touch"

The Apostle Paul tells us, in the power of the Holy Spirit, to stay well away from the concision and those who are false towards Christ. Going backwards is not an option, and we cling to the reality of Christ and not faded pictures from a past era. He is vehement about this assertion. He tells us not to touch or taste or handle these false doctrines which keep harking back to the Ceremonial law, and the worship of any entity other than God.

To practice the observance of the Old Testament ceremonial feasts and religious ceremonies, encourages the development of a legalistic mindset which becomes oppressive towards our own personal life and others. We easily become judgmental and think that everyone must adhere to the personal standards we set ourselves. We can become hard line in our thinking and gradually shut down the working of the Spirit because of our legalistic ways and strict personal judgment about what to do or not do. We are constrained to obey the moral law of God, but not the pictures of the past, which are now made reality in the coming of Christ.

This is a mindset of legalism. It looks at, tastes and handles the self-righteousness of judgmentalism and encourages salvation by works and therefore undermines our faith. We become the weaker brother, with all kinds of rules and regulations that we construct around our lives, making us slaves again to fear. The moral law stands above this and is set by God for humankind through all time. It is the peerless expression of a holy and just God, and we are duty bound to keep it with dedication. Paul is telling us to stay away from the legalism of the Old Testament covenants with God, surrounding the old life choices of the Israelites nation – the old shadows that pointed to the coming kingdom.

It starts with "looking" and progresses to "touching" this mindset of rules. We think we are becoming more holy by taking to ourselves more and more stringent "laws" about living, and then imposing them on others. God sets us free to be at liberty in our lives, and we must not become, enslaved by the unnecessary observances of laws which have passed away. We can become very judgmental and put ourselves in the slavery of these issues. We can become very obsessed with the minute details of the law and lose the liberty we have received from Christ and end up offending our own conscience.

Paul is telling us to not go near this kind of attitude and to stand firm in the faith we possess in Christ. Don't let your faith get sullied by the unfruitful works of dead laws, which Jesus has allowed to pass away.

V22 Perish

"(all of which perish with use), according to the precepts and doctrines of men?"

This translation of the verse is not very helpful. The New International translates it..

"These rules, which have to do with things that are all destined to perish with use, are based on merely human commands and teachings."

All of the ceremonial sacrifices and rituals have passed away. They are subject to time and space and are therefore fleeting reminders of a more permanent state. They have passed away. All who follow them and insist on participating in them make the Christian faith all about the outward form of things. The rituals become the most important consideration and the inner life of the soul shrinks. We place great credence on the outward and the eating, drinking and wearing of clothes, so that all our considerations are in the outer fleshly life. The ritual kills the godly mindset and arrests the development of the life of faith. The spiritual retreats and the flesh advances.

"... for the Kingdom of God is not eating and drinking, but righteousness, peace, and joy in the Holy Spirit."

Romans 14:17

All who follow the way of the outward will perish. There is nothing to be gained by outward religion, but only sin and death. The religion that God requires is the inner working of the Holy Spirit in the soul of the believer, bringing an obedient life.

Following these fleshly religious ways are also person-orientated and not of God. True worship is not about the outward form but about the inward working of the Spirit. We worship God in Spirit and in truth. All the traditions that people come up with to worship and serve, are all of no effect. Paul refutes the traditions of humankind and focuses our eyes on the inner life of the soul as we relate to God. It's the doctrine of dead works that kills the faith of the believer and brings the conscience into bondage. We get ourselves tied up in the rules and make our spiritual life of no effect.

V23 Severity

"Which things indeed appear like wisdom in self-imposed worship, and humility, and severity to the body; but aren't of any value against the indulgence of the flesh."

The outward form of religion appeals to our fleshly mindset and our love for the formality of ritual. They can seem like a good idea to us but are based on worldly wisdom and not the wisdom of God.

Worship becomes a self-imposed event with self-imposed humility therefore not sincere. We have an outward show of religion, but it is not reality in terms of God. It is not spiritual and therefore not acceptable to God. It focuses on the body and what we can present to God and not on what He has done for us – His mercy and grace which give spiritual life.

"Therefore, I urge you, brothers, on account of God's mercy, to offer your bodies as living sacrifices, holy and pleasing to God, which is your spiritual service of worship. Do not be conformed to this world, but be transformed by the

renewing of your mind. Then you will be able to test and approve what is the good, pleasing, and perfect will of God."

Romans 12:1-2

Our worship of the Lord comes from a renewed and spiritual soul, the inner workings of the Spirit of God and the heartfelt expression of sincere love. We are not to be taken in by the fleshly outworking of our unspiritual mind but have renewed minds that can test and know what is pleasing to God. Our human wisdom is set at odds with the will of God and not what He requires of us. He seeks the contrite, humble soul that will follow His wisdom and not the devices of human religious practices. All that is human is against the Lord and tends to neglect the needs of the body, and at the same time, treating it with severity in the name of this self-imposed worship. On the one hand we can be harsh in our treatment of the body, yet also neglectful. Outward religion focuses on the subjugation of the body and denying necessary needs to the body to try and bring it under a self-imposed subjection for so-called religious purposes. This is not what God requires.

In reality, the earthly religion of man is purely the indulgence of the fleshly mind and satisfies the outward expressions and not the inner work of the Spirit of God, indeed there is no worship at all, only the puffing up of the godless mind. None of it helps us in our fight against the flesh and simply serves to indulge it further and confirm us in our lack of spiritual attitudes and motivations.

Colossians Chapter Three

25 verses

Colossians Chapter Three

V1 Seek

"If then you were raised together with Christ, seek the things that are above, where Christ is, seated on the right hand of God."

The Christian is dead to the flesh and alive to Christ. When we are changed by God and brought into new life, our souls experience a resurrection, and we are made alive to God in Christ. As Jesus was raised from the dead, so our souls are raised to spiritual life in Christ and one day our bodies also. Because we are now raised to the new life, we should seek the things of that new life, the things that relate to us eternally and not to this fallen world. We seek to relate to God through the power of the Spirit and not in fleshly ways or in our natural inclinations.

Our motivation for doing so is that Christ is there in heaven, seated in glory at the right hand of God, exalted now and victorious over death and hell on our behalf. We are victorious in Him and lay hold on spiritual life because of Him. He is our rock and our fortress against the trials of life, and He is the strength of our heart.

Christ has all the authority and power over the kingdom and also over us as His people. He reigns supreme over the cosmos and over all the events and circumstances of our lives and every human life. He is the sovereign Lord and will not permit us to be lost. We possess a new life that can never be lost or stolen away from us by anyone, and we rejoice in such a great salvation.

"For I know the plans I have for you, declares the LORD, plans to prosper you and not to harm you, to give you a future and a hope. Then you will call upon Me and come and pray to Me, and I will listen to you. You will seek Me and find Me when you search for Me with all your heart."

Jeremiah 29:11-13

This is how we seek after the Lord – with all our hearts. We pray to Him and call on Him to answer our prayers for His glory and the growth of the Kingdom of God. God promises that we will find Him and know him better when we seek Him with sincerity and persistence. We seek Him in

His Word, the Scripture and we are never disappointed.

He promises that we will enter into a deeper life with Him and be conformed into the image of Christ, becoming the people we were meant to be. Jesus our Saviour and Lord will be with us to the end, for He reigns eternally over all circumstances and the people who inhabit our lives. One day we will be with Him and be raised body and soul forever with the Lord. This verse, at the beginning of chapter three in Colossians, is so full of hope and the deep truths of God and gives us confidence to live our life for God and to obey Him. We seek Him who we love, for all other loves will certainly fail, but our hope is in the risen Christ and in Him alone.

Beloved, let us seek Him with true and whole hearts, devoted to His eternal glory and in the knowledge that He will work all things out for that glory and for the good of His beloved people. We live victoriously, for the victory is already won in Christ and we enter into the reality of that victory through faith.

V2 Above

"*Set your mind on the things that are above, not on the things that are on the earth.*"

Paul is speaking plainly about our Christian life and thought processes. The godly mind is centred on Christ and the issues pertaining to God, not consumed by earthly considerations. Even as we consider our temporal lives they are viewed and planned with the will of God in sight. Those who know the Lord their God will make good judgments and their plans will be in line with what God would have in mind for His child. The better we know the Lord, the more glorifying to Him our judgments and choices will be. Our outlook on events and circumstances will be God-orientated and not just about what suits us or the people around us. God works in the lives of His people for the good of others and we live out our lives as salt and light to a decaying and darkening world.

If this is to be our lot, we must have a mind like Christ and a heart like His heart. To foster the thought processes of the Word of God and to have desires that God has, is a godly way to live. Our thoughts and deeds will not be centred around the considerations of this present world but will be for eternal aims.

The pursuit of the godly mindset is to think of the things above. We put God first in our lives and the way of righteousness, and not our own way. Then all the temporal needs and blessing will follow from His gracious provision.

"Therefore don't be anxious, saying, 'What will we eat?', 'What will we drink?' or, 'With what will we be clothed?' For the Gentiles seek after all these things; for your heavenly Father knows that you need all these things. But seek first God's Kingdom, and his righteousness; and all these things will be given to you as well."

Matthew 6:31-33

To seek the spiritual and the heavenly, is not only God honouring, but is the remedy for all worry and fretting. When our mind priorities are right, then all our needs follow on from that, for the Lord will honour those who honour Him.

"Therefore the LORD, the God of Israel, says, 'I said indeed that your house, and the house of your father, should walk before me forever.' But now the LORD says, 'Be it far from me; for those who honour me I will honour, and those who despise me shall be lightly esteemed."

1 Samuel 2:30

Here in this verse from the Old Testament, we have the alternative condition. If our mind and heart do not follow the purposes of God, we will suffer great loss. Those who are careless and remiss about their spiritual life and therefore unmindful toward the things of God will not be blessed. They will suffer the loss of the temporal blessings and lose the joy of the spiritual.

Beloved, let us watch our thought processes and stay close to the shepherd of our souls. We can live without anything, but not His gracious presence. Let us be soaked in the Word of God and obedient to His commands, thinking of all righteousness and peace.

V3 Hidden

"For you died, and your life is hidden with Christ in God."

How can we follow the ways for this fallen world and be alive to Christ?

We cannot. If we are not God-centred in our thoughts and deeds, we must seriously consider out spiritual state.

When a person is made alive in their souls, and are born again into spiritual life, we become dead to this world. It has no further interest for us or hold over us. We are set free from its deadness and the cloying effects of sin, which keep us in slavery. When we experience the life of God, this world and its attractions fade in their appeal to us, because we now have the liberty in Christ and the very power of God dwelling in our souls. If we have been enslaved by something in particular, this strength we now possess helps us to break free. God can release every chain, no matter how tightly bound we have been. Many testify to this power, and it overflows into all areas of our lives.

Why would we risk losing that power or dampening down its potency on a day-to-day basis? It would be foolish to exchange the power of God for this world's tawdry and empty promises.

So, we have died to these worldly considerations, and we are therefore now kept by that same power of God to overcome continually and persevere in our Christian lives right to the end. It is God who does this work in us, because it is His work and His will for our lives. He gives the motivation through the powerful work of the Holy Spirit who keeps us going in our life and fighting and being daily victorious.

No one or no other power can take us away from the Lord. Our lives are hidden safely in the refuge of the rock of our souls, and we are no less safe than if we were already in heaven!

"Look on my right, and see; for there is no one who is concerned for me. Refuge has fled from me. No one cares for my soul."

Psalm 142:4

Sometimes it can seem like this. Sometimes it is like this for certain people. We can find ourselves isolated so easily, but we remember we are never alone. The Lord cares for His people when all else fails. He will never leave us, even to the end. If we should find ourselves neglected, we are in the privileged position of being under God's especially care. We are precious to Him and His interest in us is direct and personal so that we always know He is in control and is actively caring for us. It is an experience not to be missed. God lifts up the downcast in a very special way and heals all our wounds.

This is the way to peace and rest in the Lord. Beloved, do not be discouraged if all things fall away from you. You are precious and gathered into His especially care under the shadow of His wings...

"The LORD is my rock, my fortress, and my deliverer, even mine; God, my rock, in him I will take refuge; my shield, and the horn of my salvation, my high tower, and my refuge. My saviour, you save me from violence. I will call on the LORD, who is worthy to be praised: So shall I be saved from my enemies."
2 Samuel 22:2-4

V4 Glory

"When Christ, our life, is revealed, then you will also be revealed with him in glory."

Here in this verse, we have the essence of the Book of Revelation. It is the comfort of the saints of God in the midst of a crooked and perverse world.

Christ Jesus has been revealed in human form at the incarnation, but one day will be fully revealed and appear in all His glory as the Lord of the worlds and every living being. Every knee will bow to Him, and all glory will be His. All those who are safe in His keeping and sheltering under His holy rule will be kept safe and will be revealed in His glory also.

Do not worry about being a person of no significance. You are a daughter or a son of the eternal kingdom and one day the Lord will put everything right. One day the skies will burst open and the Son will shine and we will not look back. The last battle will be over in an instant and the majesty of the Lord Jesus will be seen.

What a happy day that will be for every saint of God. The wrongs will melt away into the light of the kingdom come and every battle with self and sin will be finally over. We shall enter our eternal inheritance with great joy and the power of the Spirit of God will indwell us fully and fill our who souls with light. The kingdom will come it all its power and splendour and we shall reign with Christ forever. These facts ought to make a difference in our lives now, as we look forward to that time of complete renewal, when all the promises of God will be fully honoured.

We shall see our Saviour and our eternal life will begin in Him. We can enter into that reality now in the power of the Holy Spirit and know the joy of the Lord. This is our eternal destiny. Beloved, we lift our eyes off the here and now, the battles, the heartache and the disappointments and know the love of God burning in our hearts. God will bring all things to full fruition for the good and blessing of His people.

"We know that the Son of God has come, and has given us an understanding, that we know him who is true, and we are in

*him who is true, in his Son Jesus Christ.
This is the true God and eternal life."*

1 John 5:20

V5 Idolatry

"Put to death therefore your members which are on the earth: sexual immorality, uncleanness, depraved passion, evil desire, and covetousness, which is idolatry;"

Because of what Paul is saying about Christ, His appearing and our future glorified life with Him, we should put away all sinful lifestyle choices. We shut the door on our fleshly desires and put on the spiritual desires of Christ. The physical part of us must die to the desires of self and be given as a sacrifice of praise to the Saviour and Lord, as He sacrificed Himself for us and gave Himself to save us from certain death. Our souls need to be saved from the clinging sins that would dull down the beauty of spiritual life and drag us into darkness. We offer ourselves as living sacrifices to God which is our spiritual worship.

"I urge you, brothers, by the mercies of God, to present your bodies a living sacrifice, holy, acceptable to God, which is your spiritual service."

Romans 12:1

Paul gives us a list to direct our efforts into the following of the command.

Sexual immorality must be put to the death in our minds and bodies. We turn away from feeding the flesh and seeking sexual gratification. It starts in the mind and the body follows. If our mind is set on Christ, we will not succumb to the desires of the body and our cravings will cease and we will be kept pure. God gave marriage as the remedy for this set of sins and the chaste relationship of one man and one woman, living together in harmony in every part of their lives.

To live a clean life is to live to God and put away all the cravings of the fleshly life and the pursuit of ungodly ways. It means living in the power of the Spirit of God and not depending on any outside source for satisfaction. Staying away from all substance abuse, even our food and drink, and living temperate lives for God.

All depravity of every kind is far away from the mind of the Christian. We are careful what we watch and the material we put into our minds that would sully the purity of the Spirit and lead us away from the clean life lived for God.

All the range of evil desires will then be kept at bay, and we will follow the Lord in our lifestyle and in every choice that we must make. Our desires will be for the ways of God and not after the evil walk of the people who are caught up in this world. Our choices will be centred on the reality of the coming kingdom and the glory that will be revealed when this present life is over. God will make all things new and put all that is wrong to flight and make it right.

All our desire will be for the will of God and not to possess the goods of this life. We will cease seeking satisfaction in this life, which is the root of covetousness. All these considerations are idolatry and display a general hunger for the life on earth and not the spiritual life that God require or offers to us. We can be altogether too caught up with the things of this life and lose out on spiritual blessings. The flesh wars against the soul, and we must fight its effect and desires, which will one day pass away.

V6 Wrath

"...for which things' sake the wrath of God comes on the children of disobedience."

These sins that Paul is outlining are the habit and mindset of the disobedient. Those who indulge in them will suffer the full effects of the wrath of God. His wrath is poured out on the wicked, who break His commands and deliberately walk in the ways of the flesh, and not after the heart of God.

We play with the possibility of eternal punishment to our own folly. We disbelieve and cross our fingers that it is not true, playing havoc with our souls and missing the heights of delight. God's love reigns supreme and will deliver us from all evil and the effects of it on our future. Why do we turn away and embrace the pathway of foolishness and loss?

Why disobey the holy one who loves us beyond measure and will never leave us helpless or hopeless. His way is in the heavens, and He is willing and able to take us there.

The wrath of God is something to be avoided at all costs, for it is eternal and will not be deflected from the verdict of true justice. The final judgment will show the full weight of the consequences of breaking the law of God on all who refuse Him and refuse to believe. Only those who shelter in the refuge of the cross of Christ will be saved from that wrath, for we are all *"children of disobedience"* in our natural inclination. The only salvation is in Christ and in Him alone.

How we live our life and the priorities we give to the issues in our life, will show what kind of person we really are. Faith without the attending works is dead, and an empty believing will lead us to destruction.

V7 Once

"You also once walked in those, when you lived in them;"

This section of the writing dissipates any pride we might feel as redeemed people and any pet self-righteousness we might harbour. None of us can afford to look down on others, for we were once washed. None of us deserve either the temporal or spiritual blessings that we received daily. Our lives have been bought at a great price and we enjoy the things we do by the mercy of the Lord.

As we once walked in the ways of sinfulness and pride, so we lived in them, settled and secure in our godlessness and world-orientated desires. We had no inclination towards God or any desires after His holy ways but sought only our own pathway and wants. Our will was in no way compliant with God's will, and we walked blindly in the ways of this fallen world, seeking only the things we needed for happiness and personal fulfilment.

But we were rescued from this collision course with the wrath of God and made new in the renewing of our minds and will, so that we became new creations in Christ. This incredible work of salvation was not of our instigation or even desire. It is the work of God in the human heart. We do not now live as Christians after the pattern of this world, but after righteousness, because we have been changed by God. We cannot lay my claim to goodness of our own, but only what is imputed to us in Christ. We are made righteous because of His righteousness.

We walk now in humility and gratefulness for the mercy of God and the salvation which has been freely bestowed on us. We are debtors to mercy and now live our lives through the power of the Holy Spirit who resides within and are saved by the grace of God. Only when we recognise and confess this do we please the Lord. All other thoughts are self-seeking and proud.

"Don't be deceived. Neither the sexually immoral, nor idolaters, nor adulterers, nor male prostitutes, nor homosexuals, nor thieves, nor covetous, nor drunkards, nor slanderers, nor extortioners, will inherit the Kingdom of God. Such were some of you, but you were washed. But you were

sanctified. But you were justified in the name of the Lord Jesus, and in the Spirit of our God."

1 Corinthians 6:9-11

None of these sinful people will be in heaven, except they are washed clean. There is no other salvation and Jesus is the only Saviour. Beloved, we must humble ourselves and remember who we are and what we have been saved from. We walk worthy of our Saviour with thanksgiving and gratitude.

V8 Shameful

"But now you also put them all away: anger, wrath, malice, slander, and shameful speaking out of your mouth."

We can be on the Christian pathway a long time and yet fall prey to all these wrongs. We can easily be overcome, especially when we feel our needs are not being met and we are suffering. The Lord permits such things and will always supply our needs according to His riches in Christ. He will not necessarily give us all we feel we require but will meet us at our deepest human and spiritual needs and be near to us. God will give us the power to be strong in Him and to overcome as victors in Christ.

The way we speak, even to ourselves, can be an indicator of our spiritual temperature and how godly we are living our lives. The book of James is very helpful for this task of judging our speaking and vocabulary. We can all fall into bad habits, and we need the power of the Holy Spirit to keep us pure and living and speaking as we should live for the glory of God.

The Apostle Paul has another list for us here, of the heart sins that keep us away from the heat of spiritual communion with our Father in heaven. They are all inhabitants of every human heart, and we must face our part in keeping them alive in our psyche to our hurt. They must be faced and confessed and put to flight every day. No one is free from them until God makes us perfect in the coming kingdom, when Jesus will return to earth for His people, and we shall be free from the taint of all sin.

The primary sin here, is the sinful anger that cascades out of us in moments of rage. We can be so full of wrath that we lose our sense of ourselves and lose control of our Christian demeanour. Our speaking also becomes angry and shameful, and we present ourselves as out of control. It is easy to fall into this and to allow ourselves to be manipulated by other people and their mindset, and become taken in by their false living and lying ways. We must seek the pathway of Christ first and foremost in all our thinking and speaking and seek the control of the Spirit of God in every aspect of our living. Our pattern is Christ and not the way other people might present themselves to us.

The sins of the tongue are the fruit of the undisciplined mind and the inability to control what we think about and how we process events and what we hear. If we can control our tongue, then our minds are shown to be also under control and we have the ability to speak kindly and well towards others. If there is wrong things being said, we have no part in gossip, which destroys the gossip and the person being gossiped about. It is too easy to justify ourselves in this regard, and to let ourselves off the hook and give ourselves permission to speak disparagingly about other people. We can all fall into this trap, and we seek the wisdom of the Lord as we speak with friends and family to be fair and honest and not destroy a person's character in what we say about them.

Beloved, we guard our hearts with great jealousy for we are beloved of the Lord. Let no unwholesome talk come out of us, but all to the glory of God, which resides within us and will shine through in all we say and do.

V9 Practices

"Do not lie to one another, since you have taken off the old self with its practices,"

To be true to the reality of life is a challenge. There are many who are trying to live the "Christian" life, but are not true. They take to themselves a false veneer of godliness and hide behind a facade of spirituality. There are others who remain silent, hoping no one will notice them or know the truth about their life. To be sincere means we have to be honest with ourselves and face our own sins and weaknesses and deal with them. Few seem able to do so or want to do so.

The person who has become a Christian has faced their sins and confessed them to the Lord. Their life is a constant facing up and confession and change of heart and mind. This is the progress in the Christian life. Honesty in living and sincerity in what we say and do.

We may not actively tell verbal lies, but we can still be untrue, presenting ourselves as someone we are not and hiding behind a series of behaviours that we have cultivated and learned. Striving to live a holy life is the way of Christ, but it must be sincere and not just a playscript of how we have been taught to be. It is better to behave not quite rightly and be true than to play act. Admitting to yourself that you may not be quite up to the standard is a good standard and we can then face ourselves and genuinely put things right. Heartfelt repentance requires honesty with our own heart and mind.

The old self of unbelief and running from what resides in our hearts, is the old way and not the Christian way. The problem with every human heart and mind is the inability to face up to our failures and start to put that away from us for real. Change starts with recognition of the need for it, and unless we have the motivation to do so, we cannot really and truly get better.

Facing up is hard to do, but if we don't, we will continue in evil practices and our life will be a living lie. Only in Christ can we be sincere in our desire and purpose to change. Only He can make us real and the genuine article of Christian faith and love. All other striving and seeking leads to death.

Beloved, it is better to be true than a simulation of Christian virtue that is false. It is better to make mistakes than to live the Stoic life and imagine you are doing God's will. Real wisdom is learned and comes from the tutor of our souls, our Lord and God.

V10 Renewed

"…and have put on the new man, who is being renewed in knowledge after the image of his Creator,"

The old man, or the old life of self and sin has gone, and the new life in the Spirit has come. The presence of the Holy Spirit in the life of a person makes all the difference. The old life has been crucified with Christ and the new life is now lived by the power of God. The old life is dead in the grave and the new life is risen with Christ as a new life in God.

The Christian life is a constant putting off of the old self and putting on the likeness of Christ. It is a daily walk with God, becoming more like Him and learning His will and purposes for our life. We are renewed daily in the knowledge of God, what He is like and what he requires of us.

As we live from day to day in the attitude of compliance to the Lord, we learn to be like Him and to love Him. It is not a cold copying exercise, but the heartfelt following of the example of Christ and the true love of longing to be like Him. All other loves are put to flight as we focus our mind and attention on Him and succumb to His beauty and glory.

People are made in the image of God, and though we may be fallen and fail often, we can be made new in the renewing of our minds towards the Lord.

,V11 Freeman

"Where there can't be Greek and Jew, circumcision and uncircumcision, barbarian, Scythian, bondservant, freeman; but Christ is all, and in all."

There are no divisions, class structures or ungodly human social divisions in the kingdom. There is no regard for some and disregard for others. Christ is the head and Lord of all His people and no one else will trouble them. He deals with them directly and teaches and encourages them through the power of the Holy Spirit. All the constructed methods of dividing people are now defunct in the Christian church. There are no nationality issues, race issues, religious practice issues, social standing issues or relational issues. All are levelled and dealt with in Christ, and all are put aside in the name of unity and the realty of Christian fellowship.

Of course, these issues are still raised in Christian settings and there will always be divisions of all kinds, because of who we are as sinful people, but it ought not to be so. The role of prejudice in all social settings still raises its ugly head and we are still dedicated to making the divisions that suit our social settings. The tragedy today in our society, is that the church should be different, but it is not. The general society of human interaction is often fairer and more satisfying than the society we experience in the church setting. This should not be, but the church as an organisation has become bound up with corporate philosophy and the prejudicial thinking that the secular world has been fighting for years. Christian organisations and leaders have buried their heads in the sand and pretended that nothing is happening and that it does not apply to us. The result is a social arena with all sorts of factions and cliques that keep all outsiders out and condemns people to loneliness. People do not want to come among church people, because of the exclusivity of the environment and the condemnatory attitudes that dog the psyche of those who are involved there. The message is not proclaimed anyway and there is very little attempt made to reach out to others who are in any way different to the acceptable and set code of people behaviour.

Christ is not all-in-all, nor is that notion the prevailing culture of the people who go there and the mindset that they propagate. It is not biblical and not godly.

Many are staying away and finding the Christian life challenging and lonely. There is no understanding of the people who live in the real society and who are not in our church groups. Divisions abound and all sorts of sin and wrong attitudes come in. We are so hot-housed in the church culture, we don't even notice it. We might bear the name of Christ in saying we are "Christian" but we do not exhibit Him.

Our organisations become exclusive clubs for a limited type of person, and when they go, the group shrinks and one day the system will close its doors and die. This is how churches fold and fail. We do not grow because we are not preaching the gospel and people are not really changing and becoming like Christ, they are conforming to a social norm that is not real or realistic. If we refuse to change, can we really call ourselves the churches of God? The structures in place do not meet the requirements in this verse and so we are not blessed.

As individual Christians we need to ensure our attitude is that of Christ, as spoken about in this verse. We need to regard people with the dignity of Christ and as image bearers of God and not as social outcasts, however we happen to interpret that term. There are no outsiders in Christ, only dearly beloved people who have been bought at such a great price. When we start regarding each other as such, we might start to make a difference...

V12 Compassion

"Put on therefore, as God's chosen ones, holy and beloved, a heart of compassion, kindness, lowliness, humility, and perseverance;"

This is the antidote to spiritual failure. We put off the prejudice and exclusivity and put on these beautiful spiritual virtues. We have these virtues in us as God's people, and they should flow out of us in all the circumstances of our lives. We can exhibit these graces because we have been made holy and are beloved of God, therefore our hearts are full of love towards other people, especially other Christians, and we reach out with them.

Our heart should resonate with the heart of God and be in tune with His will for people and this present world. Hearts full of compassion which can empathise with other people and identify with them in sorrow and joy is the mark of the Christian. Kindness is our identity for Jesus has directly told us to be kind. We are able to humble ourselves before people of all sorts and have ceased thinking more highly of ourselves than we ought to think. Our spiritual energy is able to last out to the end of the task and carry out the will of the Father in heaven, as our Saviour did. We become more and more like Christ as we use these virtues and conform ourselves to His perfect pattern.

Having a heart of compassion is key. Without a loving heart the other graces will not follow. We will not be kind or lowly but be puffed up with the sense of our own importance and make no impact on the souls of other people. Our faith will be small, and we will be tempted to give up. Our focus will be on ourselves and how we can get people to help us, and not on making such sacrifice ourselves for other people. The inward-looking viewpoint will increase the selfish attitude that still resides in our souls and make us small-minded and self-orientated.

Only the love of Christ can sustain us and deal with our many foibles and weaknesses. It is He alone who can see His people through to the very end and save our souls from all that would drag us down. Only He can release us from a myopic view of the world and widen our outlook towards other situations other than our own.

Do not forget that we are chosen and kept in Him and through Jesus we will gain the victory. We are brave in our resistance against sin and in facing our failures for His sake. Emulating Him will make us bigger hearted and teach us to love others as we love ourselves.

V13 Forgive

"Bear with one another and forgive any complaint you may have against someone else. Forgive as the Lord forgave you."

We are to let go of all our anger and bitterness and forgive others who hurt us and freely let it all pass away from us. We are to be kind to those around us who hurt us and seek to make peace with those who even use us and put us down. We are not to offer like for like and return bad behaviour to those who dish it out. We are to be the peacemakers and the humble servants of the Lord.

This is a tall order for human beings, since naturally we are the opposite and must be taught to have regard for others.

Forgiveness is easy to think and say but hard to do. We rehearse our hurts and grievances and find it challenging to let the thoughts go that keep the resentful feelings in business. There are times that people will hurt us so badly that it damages our lives irreparably. The command then becomes more difficult than ever. There are situations that are so toxic that we have to fight to forgive but can never really fix the situation. There are people we will just have to let go of and commit our way to the Lord. There are people who become so detrimental to us that we must move away from them for the sake of our health and well-being, but the desire to harbour grudges must be dealt with in our own mind. It is all too easy for the root of bitterness to take root and determine the course of our thinking, our motivations and decisions. We can become bitter people and useless to the Lord.

When this root of unforgiveness and bitterness begins to grow, the only remedy is confession to the Lord and turning our minds deliberately to good things.

"Finally, brothers, whatever things are true, whatever things are honourable, whatever things are just, whatever things are pure, whatever things are lovely, whatever things are of good report; if there is any virtue, and if there is any praise, think about these things."

Philippians 4:8

This verse from Scripture is a great antidote for many problems in our thought life. We do not meditate on the negative but on what the Lord has done and is doing for us. The strength comes straight away, for we are obeying Him in our mind. The actions will follow our obedience in our thought life, and His comfort will come.

The terrible situations in life cannot be fixed by us, but we place our hope in the Lord that He will work all things out for our benefit and for the good of our souls. We remember and meditate on all the good He has done for us, especially in Christ in the spiritual realms and we are cheered and motivated to leave the problems to God.

Those who hurt us are also left in the hand of the Lord and He will work out all things in accordance with His holy and just will.

V14 Complaint

"...bearing with one another, and forgiving each other, if any man has a complaint against any; even as Christ forgave you, so you also do."

We are bound to forgive as we also have had need of great forgiveness.

As Christian people we are to bear with each other in our weaknesses and failures and help each other to overcome in the name of Christ. Even when other people do not understand our lives and blame us for the things that have gone wrong, we are to bear with them in love. When other people do us out and out wrong, we are to forgive them and not hold grudges against them.

If there is a situation where we have a complaint against someone we are to forgive and not make a big issue of it. There are plenty of examples where people have had to bear with us and forgive us, even things we know nothing about. It is easy to offend and be offended and it is common to want to be exonerated for situations out of our control. But often we must bear with outcomes a best we can and turn our minds to the Lord and not to the outside forces around us. We can find ourselves in impossible situations and find ourselves at the receiving end of the ill-will of other people, but we must bear with it in love and forgiveness.

Sometimes it is possible to sort out our situation and make relationships better, but sometimes it is not. People follow the way they want and often do not think about the effects of life on other people, and so many get left out and side-lined. We rise above all the foibles of human nature and trust in the Lord to see us through and give us the strength to live as he would want us to live.

Speaking personally, I am so glad to be forgiven by the Lord and for the redeeming sacrifice of Calvary and would wish to be like Him in His character and motivations. This is my prayer for all those who love the Lord and wish to be like Him.

Beloved, cast your burden on the Lord and He will sustain you. There is no one like Him and in reality, only He can know the inner workings of your heart and mind. He will bring you through the deepest of trials and make your light so shine before men that they will see your good works and glorify the Father in heaven.

V15 Peace

"And let the peace of God rule in your hearts, to which also you were called in one body; and be thankful."

We are to give way to God and allow Him to rule our hearts and lives and to be thankful to Him for all His provision. No matter how difficult it gets, He is in control and will provide for all our needs according to His riches in Christ Jesus. Sometimes we are not able to have all the things we think we need, but God knows what is best for us and will supply them so that we are sustained in our lives. Our emotions can be rather raw, but His loving kindness is always there for us. Let us rest in Him and enjoy the delights of His presence and power. He will come to us at the right time.

Where does this peace come from?

It comes from the comfort in the Word of God. We remember His word to us and rehearse it in our minds and He blesses it to our hearts. The words of other people can be comforting, but the Word of God is full of the sure and certain promises of the

Father, and He will help us to grasp them and hold them close.

It comes from a thankful heart that is grateful for all the provision of the Lord. The circumstances and situations of our lives may not be ideal, and we might lack things that we feel we need, but the Lord has provided for us and will help us. The lack of emotional support can be the most difficult to bear as we can become isolated and cut off from people we love, but the Lord is able to make it up to us and to draw close to us and let us know His comfort.

God does this through the Word of His power. To know and remember the Word of God is such a blessing and the Holy Spirit who dwells within us will bring the words to our remembrance when we need them. God will not leave us comfortless but will come to us. He will make up the lack of other people and the sweetness of His love will surround us. We are thankful for the Word of God and all His provision, in our temporal lives too.

We are called to peace in the body of Christ also. There should be family love between sisters and brothers in Christ and the support of each other in our needs. It can be difficult to find a church where there is the family feeling and the friendly support we all need, young and older. To find it is precious, and also the faithful teaching of the Scripture so that we are comforted in it and grow up in Christ.

Beloved, let us dwell in peace at all times and not fret, for it disturbs our peace and takes away our faith in the Lord. Let us live quietly and peaceably and know His support each day and have loving hearts full of devotion to Him and full of faith.

V16 Singing

"Let the word of Christ dwell in you richly; in all wisdom teaching and admonishing one another with psalms, hymns, and spiritual songs, singing with grace in your heart to the Lord."

It can be much easier to remember words when they are set to a tune. The rhyme structure in hymns is very helpful to remember and the words can be a great comfort to us as we say them in our head or sing them. It is wonderful how they come to mind at the right time and how God can bring words to our remembrance to help us in the situations of life.

The practice of learning Scripture by heart is also extremely helpful for it will come back into the mind at the right time. God will bring these things to our mind, so that the Holy Spirit can use them for our glory and encouragement. We also encourage each other with these words and bring them to our memory and rehearse the truths of God in Scripture and in verse.

Singing is such a great activity. It exercises the mind, the heart and voice to the glory of God. It lifts the spirits and cheers the gloomy days with the joy of the Lord. We can sing or listen to Christian music which lifts our mind to the Lord.

Should we listen to Christian music only?

This is a delicate issue. We should listen to what is helpful to us and encourages us in the Lord. Sometimes secular music can be helpful, and it soothes the troubled mind and soul, but much of it has unhelpful lyrics that can make our heart cold and divert our attention to something else rather than the truths of God. Too much of it will affect our mindset and divert our thinking into ungodly ways and thought patterns. The secular words will drown out the Word of God and we will find ourselves singing and reciting the words of the godless sentiments that are not helpful to our soul.

We encourage each other in the Lord and put His truth first and foremost in our lives and we will reap the harvest of comfort and good cheer. This will reinforce the grace of God towards us and be a constant reminder of our dear Saviour and friend and all that He means to us. If we entertain the ungodly words and music, it will not benefit us much and will indeed take us away from thinking about the Lord and all that He is and has done for us.

The constant sound of romance songs is very unhelpful and will divert out thinking to things we don't need to consider or rehearse. They can take us away from the reality of the love relationships in our life and concoct a false kind of thinking about what love is. We can find ourselves thinking falsely about love and live our thought life in a fantasy land, which is detrimental to our psyche and the reality of love in our life. We rehearse the things of God and the realities of the spiritual life, which will strengthen our soul and fill us with good thoughts and the remembrances of the truths of God. This bolsters up the mind and heart and will help us to fight temptation and sin that would overtake our life and cause of hurt.

"Let the word of Christ dwell in you richly.."

We do all we can to propagate the Word deep in our soul and keep our mind as the mind of Christ.

V17 All

"Whatever you do, in word or in deed, do all in the name of the Lord Jesus, giving thanks to God the Father, through him."

Everything we think and say and do should be captured to Christ. It is a great regulator of our words and deeds to know we do them all in the name of the Lord Jesus. We can find ourselves rehearsing our griefs and failures and getting ourselves in a bad spiritual state by forgetting what God has done for us and in us. We forget that we are redeemed people, and the past is all forgiven by the Lord, and we have been given a new start. Every time we fall, the Lord is there to correct us and pick us up and set us on our feet again. What a loving Saviour and Companion He is! He loves us with no regard for our past sins. They are forgotten in the sea of forgetfulness. He has paid the price already and we are free people. But our thoughts and words can bind us again in the bonds of blame and confusion. Let us put away the words and deeds that would separate us from the Lord our God and walk worthy lives for His glory and our own good.

We can be so cruel to ourselves, and we can allow others to call the shots in our thought processes. We must cling to the words of the Scripture and not the lies of the enemy, or the blame of other people. We look to our Saviour and are so thankful for all that He has done for us. He has set us free, and we must never forget that.

Everything we do is for His sake and remembering that His yoke is easy and His burden light. He is not a taskmaster nor is He harsh in His treatment of us. Unfortunately, we are often harsh on ourselves and sometimes on each other too.

"The merciful man does good to his own soul, but he who is cruel troubles his own flesh."

Proverbs 11:17

We must remember our own flesh and its limitations and weaknesses and not be unkind in our judgment of ourselves. We avoid sin and fight the unrighteousness that is in us, but we must not make our lives harsh and difficult and full of misery. The Lord gives us all things to richly enjoy, and all His things are ours in Christ. A cruel person is cruel to themselves, and this should not be the case, because the Lord is not cruel to us. Too many rules and regulations about life and a tight and unyielding legalistic spirit can make us so dull and restrictive. We stop enjoying life and start to pile on the blame and guilt. Christ our Lord has set us free from all that, so let us stand fast in His liberty and enjoy the life He has graciously given us to enjoy. We give thanks to Him for it and express our gratefulness to Him for all He does in us, by living our life for His glory and praise.

As we praise and thank our Father in heaven through the Lord Jesus Christ, so we give the glory to the right cause and set our priorities right, and our minds are focused on the right things. God will reward us and give us peace and the felt sense of His presence with us. We will find we have the strength to say and do the right thing when the time comes for us to act and speak.

"Settle it therefore in your hearts not to meditate beforehand how to answer, for I will give you a mouth and wisdom which all your adversaries will not be able to withstand or to contradict."

Luke 21:14-15

If we give Him all, words and deeds, we
will reap a rich harvest...

V18 Fitting

"Wives, be in subjection to your husbands, as is fitting in the Lord."

It is really important who we marry. We must choose a partner prayerfully and with great wisdom. It is a one-time choice and should reflect the love relationship between Christ and His church. Our behaviour in marriage should be fitting in the Lord and reflect the love relationship between the persons of the godhead and the love of Christ for His redeemed people. The relationship is one of mutual love and submission.

Wives are to relate to their husbands as the church relates to Christ. This presumes the husband is like Christ and is a loving and sacrificial man who will put the well-being of his wife above himself.

Women especially must be careful who they marry, since many interpret the word "submission" as women being underlings and must do what the husband says. There are still too many who treat their wives as chattels or as housekeepers giving special privileges to them, and not as people with dignity and purpose and a personal life with God. It should be a loving relationship with both parties willing to acquiesce to each other for we are yet sinful people and not infallible.

The Bible teaches mutual submission and the living and constant respect for each other as people and as individual people at that. The wife is not the same as the husband and decisions should be made together and with mutual consent. Where there is no consent, it is oppression and abuse and worse.

"Subjecting yourselves one to another in the fear of Christ."

Ephesians 5:21

We are to practice submission as is fitting in the Lord, not a craven fear of one party or the other, or of one lording it over the other. Marriage is not a chopping block or a pity party for the man to be bolstered up in his psyche and ego and given Carte Blanche to dictate the terms of every discussion or decision. There must be sharing. Without sharing there is no caring and the oppressed party will eventually give way in disappointment and will give up on the "relationship" which can turn out to be no relationship at all.

Marriage is very difficult and should not be entered into lightly. Both parties should be sure that God is directing them, and decisions should be made prayerfully and with due regard for each other in each other's life.

Women should be thoughtful about whether marriage is for them at all, since many are very able and have their own life ideas and desires. It is very difficult to give this all up to be a pick-up person for a man, who requires a stultifying submission and complete acquiescence. It should not be like this, but it often is or works out that way in practice.

This will not work for many women, and many spend life under achieving and miserable about their state. The man ends up abusing the wife and putting down her wishes and desires and so how can a marriage be happy and fruitful? This will affect the children and cause a lot of difficulties and develop bad thinking and feelings. We must consider the long-term view of marriage and not the short-term gain of having a companion.

Marriage means giving all and we become a part of each other. Women have to decide what kind of relationship they want in their life, or whether they would be better off alone. There are many ways to have family and friends and marriage is only one state of being.

There are plenty of examples where subjection is not fitting in the Lord, and we should consider this in all our doing and being. Putting people down and ruling over free people with impunity is not godly and blaming others for what goes wrong and not examining ourselves, is a skill we all need to learn. Marriage is a learning experience, and we need to be sure we choose someone who will learn with us and be prepared to change and grow. The way I personally have observed marriages in churches is not heart-warming and I see a lot of rejection and neglect against women. This is not pleasing to the Lord, and the dirth of responsibility for the elements in the marriage is woeful. Something must be done, for women are suffering and are staying out of church because of toxic relationships.

We must learn mutual submission, or all is lost and the beautiful picture of marriage on the Scripture will be lost for future generations, and we are left with a cultural equivalent that damages women and also men in the long term.

V19 Love

"Husbands, love your wives, and don't be bitter against them."

Love holds all things together, but it must be real and sincere. There is a godless Stoicism that will just doggedly keep on going, grit the teeth and carry on. It is not love or devotion and is hiding the real situation that can never be sorted out. It makes a marriage into a lie.

Husbands are especially targeted here in this verse for especial reminder that they must truly love their wives and not descend into the bonds of duty in marriage. If marriage is to last it must be true. We must make up our minds at the start what we want, and we must work to ensure that our relationships stay honest and righteous.

It is too easy to become bitter and to become a hyper-critical spouse and men seem to be more prone to this. The Apostle Paul is reminding the men in the marriage relationship to pay close attention to being sincere and genuine in their love relationships and to truly love their wives as they love themselves.

Women can do many things that men find difficult, and it is easy to side-line these skills and ignore the relational aspect of life and focus on the practical. It is too easy to denigrate someone who can do the things you cannot and to put our spouses down and side-line their abilities and gifts. If marriage is to be rich and successful, it must have the full love and devotion of both parties. Without this love, the marriage will eventually die. A person can hide and pretend but it will not last the ravages of life and the pressures put on relationships by the outside world. Love will conquer all and will overcome all obstacles and shine brightly as something everyone can look to and gain strength from. This is also what builds families and helps our children and grandchildren to grow. Fake devotion can never succeed because it is dishonest. True hearts will stay together and win the day with true devotion and faithfulness. Love wins.

V20 Obey

"Children, obey your parents in all things, for this pleases the Lord."

Children in the family must have resect and obey their parents, as commanded by the Lord.

"Honour your father and your mother, that your days may be long in the land which the Lord your God gives you."

Exodus 20:12

It is for the peacefulness of the family and the development of the character of the children that they regard their parents and do what they are asked. It is a blessing to be brought up in a godly household where the law and God and the love of God are worked out in the life of the family. It is more difficult if you are outside that experience, but the grace of God calls all kinds of people to Himself.

It is important that we learn to respect our parents so that we can have some semblance of understanding of what it is to regard the Lord and obey Him.

Obedience is pleasing to the Lord and was the defining feature of the life of Jesus Christ. He was obedient to the Father and obeyed all the commandments and the pathway that was set out for Him, that all righteousness might be fulfilled.

"And being found in human form, he humbled himself, becoming obedient to death, yes, the death of the cross."

Philippians 2:8

There was no other obedient like Him, that He might be our example and advocate before the Father. We put on the robes of His righteousness because we have none of our own. We learn to obey the Lord, whether we had an upright beginning in life or not. Obedience pleases the Lord, so we must teach our children obedience and to conform to the authority over them. We also encourage each other to conform to the obedience and image of Christ, that we also will be righteous people who please the Lord.

V21 Don't

"Fathers, don't provoke your children, so that they won't be discouraged."

The perfect follow up to the preceding verse. Children should obey, but parents must not put unnecessary burdens in their children. It is easy to allow the weight of legalism to infiltrate our families and we construct all kinds of perfunctory rules and regulations, which are really just a tool to control. It is an ungodly mindset and undermines the ability of children to choose the right things for themselves. It makes them dependent on the parent and takes away their own sense of themselves and the prospect of a personal relationship with God.

The innate human desire to tell people what to do, can overcome us in various roles in our life, and none more so than in parenting. To be over-bearing toward the child in the upbringing of that child causes insecurities and lack of personal confidence. It encourages dependence on us as fragile human beings, and not on the living and true God who is searching for His children. To be too light-handed in the upbringing of the children, can encourage lawlessness and rebellion, which can also come from being too dictatorial also.

We work out the upbringing of our children with fear and trembling and dependant on the grace and mercy of the Lord to direct our paths and bring our children safely into the heavenly fold. We should be more encouraging of them rather than the constant correction and punishment that some families follow. This is not helpful to the child. It could also tip quite easily into abuse and taking away the fundamental rights of the child.

We aim for godly, faithful, sincere relationships that guide our children into all truth, but realising that we cannot dictate their final characters or personalities but leave that in the loving hands of God. Perhaps less is more. Perhaps a lighter touch is better than the heavy hand. God lets us make mistakes so that we can learn from them, and in all things leads us into all truth. Families should operate in this way too, and make independent and confident learners, who know the Lord and will walk with Him in courage and obedience, as we also should as clear examples of God's handiwork.

V22 Servants

"Servants, obey in all things those who are your masters according to the flesh, not just when they are looking, as men pleasers, but in singleness of heart, fearing God."

We are not talking here of being sycophants who acquiesce to all requests and try to be people-pleasers. We are to be sincere in our work and do it properly at all times, when we are being observed and when we are not. We are to carry out the duty requests of our managers and bosses with a good heart, thoroughly and with a happy spirit. We have one purpose in all things, to please the Lord. When we do our work well, the Lord is glorified, whoever sees it or not. In all our tasks we set out to be honest and sincere and that includes when we work at a job we do not like or for someone who is oppressive. The Lord refines our attitudes as we do His will and obey the Scripture whether we feel like it or not.

If we are asked to do something which is against our conscience, we can speak up, even when is costs us, or puts our future in jeopardy. God will honour what we do and will protect us. If we have been honest and true at work, then it is easier to speak up, because it will be known that we are not trouble-makers but sincere. Sometimes it will cause suffering to us and sometimes we will see the delivering hand of God in our circumstances. In all things we trust Him and stick closely to the holy commandments.

We may not be actual servants, but we all serve in some capacity, even if it is family and friends. We serve gladly and with a good heart to ensure the comfort of those we serve. We all serve each other in Christ, and no one is above another. Indeed, the more recognition we receive, the greater the servant we become.

"In that hour the disciples came to Jesus, saying, "Who then is greatest in the Kingdom of Heaven?" Jesus called a little child to himself, and set him in the middle of them and said, "Most certainly I tell you, unless you turn and become as little children, you will in no way enter into the Kingdom of Heaven. Whoever therefore humbles himself as this little child is the greatest in the Kingdom of Heaven."

Matthew 18:1-4

To be great in the eternal kingdom of Christ we must become the servant of all. This goes against our human and fleshly desires, and we find it difficult to put ourselves in the low position and keep ourselves there. We prefer to be recognised and lauded and made to feel we are important. But the way of Christ is very different to this world, and if we are to live for Him, we need to be prepared for that. We gain all our confidence and encouragement from Him and those we know who also love Him and are His servants.

V23 Heartily

"And whatever you do, work heartily, as for the Lord, and not for men,"

Here in this verse, we have the reinforcement of the sentiment to work hard as unto the Lord. If we have this attitude, it will make our difficult work sweet and our labours a blessing to us. All things, as unto the Lord. It will then cease to matter who we work for or what they are like, for our eternal Father watches over us and knows what we can bear. He is moulding and making our character, and the circumstances of our life are His express interest and design. What family we are involved with and what job we do, are all under His choosing. Even the difficulties of life and the stresses and strains are under this jurisdiction. Nothing is outside His control, although we might think it is! The sovereignty of God interfaces all our life and will direct our footsteps to the end. We cannot make a mistake, for His guiding hand will keep us and sustain us as we learn our lessons and walk daily with Him.

What if the manager or person in charge is unreliable?

Our hearts do not change whoever is our director in this life. We do all for the glory of God and with a happy and joyful heart, no matter what the circumstances. Perhaps the people around us are untrustworthy, but we pray for them that they will be released from their bonds and find the liberty in Christ that we now have by the grace of God. None of us have any hope without the Lord and we should have some sympathy for those who oppress us, as they are also oppressing Christ and are therefore not in a good state in this world or in the judgment of God. This is impossible for us to feel unless the same Spirit of love is at work in our heart as is in the heart of Jesus. It is easy to be bitter, but we are not of that type. We pray for those who oppose us and put us down. God will deliver us from the grasp of the wicked at the right time and will bless our faithfulness and witness to them.

"But I tell you, love your enemies, bless those who curse you, do good to those who hate you, and pray for those who mistreat you and persecute you, that you may be children of your Father who is in heaven. For he makes his sun to rise on the evil and the good, and sends rain on

the just and the unjust. For if you love those who love you, what reward do you have? Don't even the tax collectors do the same? If you only greet your friends, what more do you do than others? Don't even the tax collectors do the same? Therefore you shall be perfect, just as your Father in heaven is perfect."

Matthew 5:44-48

If we enjoy good governance over us, we give thanks to God and do our work well so that all may see our good works and glorify God. To live and work in such a godly frame of mind is life and peace and we will live our lives in a perfect frame of mind, even as the Lord Jesus did. He is our pattern and our praise...

V24 Rewards

"…knowing that from the Lord you will receive the reward of the inheritance; for you serve the Lord Christ."

When we think of the rewards that are ahead and the inheritance we have in Christ, it should enervate us to have the motivation to serve the Lord with gladness in our situation. Too often we do not mediate on our spiritual blessings in Christ and are too earth bound in our search for meaning and significance. We value the good pleasure of others before the *"well done"* of the Lord. Someday, the people of God will receive the fruit of their labours for the Lord, from His gracious hand. It will be personal, and we will receive the words of commendation if we have persevered to the end and overcome our worldly disposition.

One day the trials of our life will all pass away and the petty troubles we have experienced will evaporate into the glory of the Lord. We will enter into the full light of the redemption that has been bought for us at Calvary and we will receive the inheritance we have been promised in

Christ. Our earth-bound trials will cease and we will forget them.

"For our light affliction, which is for the moment, works for us more and more exceedingly an eternal weight of glory, while we don't look at the things which are seen, but at the things which are not seen. For the things which are seen are temporal, but the things which are not seen are eternal."

2 Corinthians 4:17-18

The remedy for our present troubles is to lift our eyes away for them and gaze deeper into the inheritance from God. We can see it in the Holy Scriptures and by faith lay hold on it and are encouraged. If we are unclear about what that inheritance is or what is laid up for us in heaven, we can get a clear view from Ephesians chapter One. We have here a list of our spiritual blessings in Christ which we can access even now and enjoy. We are guilty of forgetfulness, and we look to the temporal blessings in life for validation and encouragement, which they cannot give us in the long term. They are temporary stop gaps to bless us, but they can never satisfy the soul that longs for Christ.

Beloved, as we serve the Lord Christ, let us remember what He requires of us, that we walk in faith and devotion to Him. As our sight is lifted to higher ground, we are given better motivation to walk worthy of the Lord, than the fleeting rewards of this life.

Our inheritance is kept for us above and one day we will fully enter into it. No one can take it away and no circumstance in life will spoil what has been stored away. God will renew all things and open all doors for us, so that we will serve Him with all the powers He has given to us and strengthen our hold on spiritual life. Let us hold on in faith and hope to all He has given to us and continue to serve Him in the life that He has allotted to us.

V25 Partiality

"But he who does wrong will receive again for the wrong that he has done, and there is no partiality."

God does not have favourites, but he does have His own people who he loves with an everlasting love. God does not treat us as our sins deserve. We receive full and free forgiveness from His mercy and everlasting life as a free gift of His grace.

However, if we sin and sin wilfully, we will suffer consequences in our lives. God will not allow us to run on in our sinfulness without there being some kind of chastisement. The child of God will act and react and seek the Lord again. There is redemption for our backsliding, but there are often life situations that we must deal with and difficulties we will have to face up to.

Sin in the life of the Christian is serious, for it stops the blessing of God and separates us from the close fellowship we all seek and need. God will not allow it to continue and will find a way to stop it and bring us back into the fold once more. We wander away at our peril and are vulnerable to ravenous people who would destroy our faith and lead us away from God. In our life circumstances we need the protecting hand of God and His over-ruling purpose that will guide us and keep us in the heavenly way.

The Lord our Saviour does not punish us, for all punishment was swallowed up on the cross and there is no more condemnation for the Christian. But there are outcomes of bad decisions and sinful mindsets that must be faced.

In all situations and relationships, the Lord does not treat us as our sins deserve but pours out mercy towards us and binds up our hurts and heals our broken hearts. He does not favour one of His children above another and will work out all things for the good of each one, according to His purposes. His love is everlasting, and His grace extends to us in our need and fallen-ness.

The Lord is faithful to us even if we are unfaithful and will never let us go beyond the bounds of His will for us. Even our sinfulness is written into the plan, and He can work all things out for good in a way that no one else can. In this time, we commit our way to Him and stay away from the sin that would lead us away from Him and earnestly seek to stay close to our Father in heaven who loves us with an everlasting love.

Colossians Chapter Four

18 verses

Colossians Chapter Four

V1 Equal

"Masters, give to your servants that which is just and equal, knowing that you also have a Master in heaven."

This is the instruction to balance the faithfulness of the servant to the master. Masters must also treat servants equitably and fairly. They must have respect for what they do, and for who they are as people. Managers and bosses are put in a position of trust with a duty of care over the people who work for them, and it is all too easy to take advantage of workers and abuse them.

"You shall not oppress your neighbour, nor rob him. The wages of a hired servant shall not remain with you all night until the morning."

Leviticus 19:13

How we treat those who work for us is very important as it shows our attitude to both ourselves and the workforce. If we think we are successful in our own efforts, we will become proud and imagine we can treat people as we see fit. If we are greedy, we will be willing to build our success on the back of others with little recompense or recognition. If we are mean, we will be unable to share the good things that we are able to have.

God has given all for us. He did not hold back the sacrifice of His own beloved Son that we as sinners should not perish in our sins. How can we take advantage of others knowing what was given for us?

God is our Master and will recompense us according to what we have done. We must also recompense others fairly as we also would like to be treated by God. The measure we judge others is the measure by which we also will be judged. If we take unfairly from the efforts of other people, we will lose out in our eternal reward. There are those who will be saved by the skin of their teeth and will have no reward. The way we operate in this life as Christian people is very important. Taking what is not ours has serious consequences, even in this life. A bad reputation can ruin our labours and render our work useless. We should be imbursing those who serve us in an appropriate manner and giving them the opportunities to improve and make progress in life.

"Don't judge, so that you won't be judged. For with whatever judgment you judge, you will be judged; and with whatever measure you measure, it will be measured to you."

Matthew 7:1-2

Fairness in all things. We should find ourselves judging on the side of generosity rather than short measures, as this is the way of the Christian. God will honour those who honour His ways and standards, and those who are evil will not succeed in the long run. We lay up treasure in heaven, not in this fallen doomed earth.

V2 Continue

"Continue steadfastly in prayer, watching therein with thanksgiving;"

We must pray and not cease...

The Apostle instructs us to continue in prayer and to not give up. We pray and watch for answers and the over-arching will of God in all things. We should know the mind of God so that we can ascertain what His will would be because we know his character so well. We can see the work of His will in our own life and therefore get to know His purposes for us and how He works in the life of other people as well. This will inform our prayers and we will pray according to his will, and He will hear us.

As we watch for the outworking of our prayers and the will of God we will be filled with thanksgiving. Thanksgiving is the burning fuel of the Christian life. It enervates and powers all the praise, worship, service and love for the Lord Jesus. The grateful heart continually rehearses the mercies it has received, and this feeds the constant flow of thankful prayer to God. Gratefulness is the fountain head of the power of God in the life of the Christian. The constant flow of it wears away the rock of the hardness of our heart and makes it conform to the will and purpose of the Lord and not the selfishness of our own way.

As we then pray, we will be looking for the outworking of answers to our prayers with joy and faith. As we see the answers to our prayers, we will give thanks in gratitude to the mercy shown to us that God should include us in his will in this way. We will have the victory over the gloom that naturally infests our minds and will rejoice in God our Saviour.

"Always rejoice. Pray without ceasing. In everything give thanks, for this is the will of God in Christ Jesus toward you."

1 Thessalonians 5:16-18

This is the key to the victory over sin and temptation in the Christian life. It is the path of rejoicing and the living of a life full of gratitude to the Lord for all His love. This is the will of God for every Christian and the powerhouse of the overcomer. Continue in prayer...

V3 Open

"...praying together for us also, that God may open to us a door for the word, to speak the mystery of Christ, for which I am also in bonds;"

This is what we live for as Christian people. To speak the Word of Christ. Either using voice or the written word, we seek to tell the sinner about the reality of forgiveness and a new life, and the saint, the building up of faith and love. We pray that God will open doors for us to speak for Him and we take every opportunity that He affords us to spread the good news about Jesus. We pray for each other that we will have the courage and knowledge to speak when we get a hearing and the ability to make the most of every opportunity to comfort people with the love of Christ.

We speak the mystery of Christ. It is a mystery because it is not from the human psyche, and therefore cannot be understood without the Spirit of God teaching us. The message is from God and relates His love for us when we were still His enemies and dead to His voice, He died for us. No one else would do such a thing for us and no one else will love ignoble us. Though we are far from God, He reaches out to us and calls us to come to Him personally and repent of our sin. We can know the freedom from its stultifying bonds, as a gift from God. God is willing to give us total forgiveness for everything and eternal life when this life is over. The love of God knows no bounds and He offers it freely to us. The mystery is His sacrificial love that will hold us fast and bring us safely home to heaven. There is no other gospel and no other salvation.

The Apostle Paul sought to speak this message at every chance he would get and asks the believers at Colosse to pray for open doors to do so. He is in prison at this point and so his opportunities seem limited, but God is able to deliver his servant and raise him up to speak again. Even in prison Paul is reaching out to the Christians in the churches and writing the letters, of which this is one. Perhaps he is thinking of the door of the prison opening for him, so that he can visit the churches again and further spread the gospel. Perhaps he knows this is the end of the line for him but is encouraging us to take up the torch of truth and run with it.

Beloved, do we pray for each other in this way? Do we seek to be useful to Christ and be adept at speaking for Him? We put our trust and confidence in the Lord and know that He will help us as we step up to witness for Him. As God opens the door, so we can go through it and make the most of our opportunities to make a difference for Christ and be ambassadors for His sake.

V4 Reveal

"…that I may reveal it as I ought to speak."

There are times when our attitude may not be right, and we lack love towards other people and speak out of turn or out of tone. Paul asks for prayer that this will not be true of him.

He also seeks to have the ability to share the gospel fully and openly to show the whole message of God and His plan for sinful people. Paul seeks the confidence that comes from God to preach the gospel with the authority that it should have. Nothing must be hidden or apologetically explained but put forward as the Word of God and the only way for the forgiveness of sins and the daily walk of fellowship with the Lord.

There are times when we can be over-awed by our audience and intimidated by the people we are around, and so we soft-pedal the message, not wishing to offend. We must fight the urge to water down the gospel so that it is more acceptable to the fallen human psyche. We are not to hide any part of it or save ourselves from the embarrassment of giving negative information. We need to reveal the gospel as it is portrayed for us in the holy scripture and preach it from the scripture.

The classic side-step is the reality of the punishment of God to all those who refuse to repent and believe. It is very offensive to the human mind that God should have that kind of right over us. We believe and are taught in self-determination, and the fact that God is in control, offends us greatly. We need to ask for the courage and strength to stick to the message and not be put off by social considerations. Losing friends is a distinct possibility but you will have told them the truth and God will ensure the sharing of His Word will bless and save the lost.

As the message is revealed in the Scripture so we reveal it to others around us, and especially those who preach it from the front.

"For if I preach the Good News, I have nothing to boast about; for necessity is laid on me; but woe is to me, if I don't preach the Good News."

1 Corinthians 9:16

The messenger of the Lord is compelled to preach the Good News of the gospel in all its glory and fulness. There are warnings against not sounding out this aspect of warning to people, about the wrath of God to come against all who wickedly refuse salvation.

"When I tell the wicked, You shall surely die; and you give him no warning, nor speak to warn the wicked from his wicked way, to save his life; the same wicked man shall die in his iniquity; but his blood will I require at your hand. Yet if you warn the wicked, and he doesn't turn from his wickedness, nor from his wicked way, he shall die in his iniquity; but you have delivered your soul."

Ezekiel 3:18-19

This is the warning against not sounding out the warning! We are naturally reticent to do so, but the Lord will help us at the right time and in the right way as the Apostle has prayed for.

V5 Redeeming

"Walk in wisdom toward those who are outside, redeeming the time."

God constrains us to be wise and to live wisely in our lives before all people. We do this because time is short, and we do not know how long we have allotted to us. We see his glory in our lives and want to meet Him one day, with treasure stored up in that heavenly place. We don't know how many people we will be able to influence and witness to for Christ, so all things must be brought under the subjection of a godly life. We seek the wisdom only God can give to live and speak for Him, and to be honest and sincere in all we are as God's people.

Perhaps we have wasted a lot of time procrastinating and backsliding one way or another, and we need to get the discipline back in our lives to live for Christ. We do this through devotion to the person of Christ, realising that He is a person, and we relate to him as a person. We do this through the Word of God and daily meditations on the Word to discover more and more about our God and Saviour JESUS the Lord. As we get to know Him more fully, we ask for the wisdom of God with a clearer view of what that is. Then we can walk in the ways of wisdom and be wise people in the Lord.

"This I say therefore, and testify in the Lord, that you no longer walk as the rest of the Gentiles also walk, in the futility of their mind... But you did not learn Christ that way; if indeed you heard him, and were taught in him, even as truth is in Jesus: that you put away, as concerning your former way of life, the old man, that grows corrupt after the lusts of deceit; and that you be renewed in the spirit of your mind, and put on the new man, who in the likeness of God has been created in righteousness and holiness of truth."

Ephesians 4:17-24

We put off the old way of life that feeds off a futile and unwise mind and put on Christ. We learn from Him in humility and peaceable-ness, denying the uncleanness of self and greed, and are renewed daily. We seek wisdom, righteousness, holiness and truth, not just to satisfy ourselves with the things of this life and the desires of our earthy selves. If we live according to righteousness, we will necessarily be happy, for the Lord will bless us in our inner souls and others will see the difference from what we used to be and how we are different from the world around us. Our witness will be strong for it will be sincere.

If we are living rightly then we have the opportunity and authority to speak right too. Otherwise, we are simply hypocrites who deny the power of the Holy Spirit and have no real faith in the ways of God. Christians are not like other people, and if they are, they are not!

Ignorance of God breeds lack of understanding and so hardness of heart ensues. No one will be attracted by this and no semblance of the love of God will be seen in us. It's all or nothing. A life of faith or the life of unbelief.

Beloved, let us redeem the time, lest we waste the time. There is so much at stake for eternity, so let us walk worthy of our Lord Jesus.

V6 Seasoned

"Let your speech always be with grace, seasoned with salt, that you may know how you ought to answer each one."

Our marker for how we are is the way we speak, to ourselves and other people. Our words betray our mindset for good or bad. If we are talking with ourselves and reasoning about or situation and other people, our inner speech should be gracious, remembering we are heard by the Lord. We might think we can be "ourselves" in private, but it is too easy to be hypocritical. We think negative thoughts about others in our private places in our heads, and speak differently about them, as is socially acceptable. Which is true?

God sees our inner life up close and clearer than we do, and it behoves us to pay more careful attention to our private lives.

"Anyone who doesn't stumble in word is a perfect person, able to bridle the whole body also."

James 2:3

If we are in control of what we say, we are in control. This includes the private conversations we have with ourselves. It is difficult to patrol the various areas of our psyche. How careful we are and how persistent, betrays our efforts in godliness. We blow hot and cold and still our loving God holds us fast.

We must practice using the seasoning of the Word of God to remind us and teach us how we should be. Applying it to our lives and specifically our speech is our daily task. Watching our private speech will automatically improve our public speech and our general mindset. The Apostle is instructing us that our speaking should be gracious and helpful to the hearer, and not destructive or encourage ill will or bad feelings.

This can be a difficult skill because there are times we have to speak plainly and point out the bad things that are happening around us, but that also is an acquired skill born of the Spirit of God. It is our attitude to others that is key. We speak to improve their situation and build the other person up, not to continually knock them down. Even as we criticise it is seasoned with the salt of the grace of God and the power of the Holy Spirit.

"Let no corrupt speech proceed out of your mouth, but such as is good for building up as the need may be, that it may give grace to those who hear. Don't grieve the Holy Spirit of God, in whom you were sealed for the day of redemption. Let all bitterness, wrath, anger, outcry, and slander, be put away from you, with all malice. And be kind to one another, tenderhearted, forgiving each other, just as God also in Christ forgave you."

Ephesians 4:29-32

V7 Known

"All my affairs will be made known to you by Tychicus, the beloved brother, faithful servant, and fellow bondservant in the Lord."

What trust the Apostle Paul is able to have in the Christian believers in Colosse! Could this be true of a local church in our day? Are we able to have the confidence in each other that we judge kindly and positively and are open and sincere?

The Apostle had an open account with the Christians churches in his day and could be trusted by everyone to do and say the right thing. He was such a man of God and so faithful to the heavenly vision and the Word of God. His wisdom was peerless and he had an answer for everyone. This is because he also kept short accounts with the Lord and kept his life daily perfect before God. Every sin was confessed and expunged and so his life was holy. He could tell the Christians to be like him, because he was like Christ.

"Be imitators of me, even as I also am of Christ."
1 Corinthians 11:1

The attitude and life of Paul was open to the scrutiny of others and he was able to live this life by the power of God. The same Spirit of God dwells in every Christian, so why is there such falling away and apostasy in our days? We have lost the attitude of godliness and excuse our sin and do not seek the perfect life of God. We excuse ourselves by saying that Paul was special, but he was saved in the same way as everyone else and is just a son of the kingdom like everyone else too. The search of holiness will lead us in the way of Paul and of Christ.

Paul was obviously keen that the other brothers in Christ should report about what he was doing to the other churches and continued his life as a living testimony to the grace of God. Paul did not hide from people, but freely conversed and wrote to them many letters of teaching, encouragement and news about what he was doing. His accountability was universal, and every Christian could know about what he did. His letters were to the churches and were read to the churches so that everyone could see and be clear about what Paul thought and did.

Paul's witnesses were also solid and reliable people. He calls Tychicus his beloved brother, faithful servant and fellow bondservant in the Lord. Paul had many who lived and worked like this, a far cry from the celebrity preachers and pastors we have nowadays. The work these men of God did was sacrificial, hard and cost them their lives in the end. They relied on the love of God rather than the acclaim of men and on the faithfulness of the Lord rather than the fickleness of the human heart. They did not play to the gallery but were honest and sincere and took the place of humility rather than fame and fortune.

What would happen if we were to live like that today? Perhaps we instinctively know that it would not necessarily go well with us. Look what happened to the Christians in the early church and to our Lord Jesus Christ...

Beloved, let us put on courage and faith as we step out and step up for God. May we live our lives in holiness and honesty before the people God has put around us, and make ourselves as the example of our dear brother, Paul and our Saviour JESUS.

V8 Purpose

I am sending him to you for this very purpose, that he may know your circumstances and comfort your hearts,"

The sense of openness in the early church was so striking. There were no divisions and the Christians shared with each other sacrificially and continually as there was need. Paul is sending Tychicus to the church in Colosse to find out what they needed and to comfort them in whatever way they needed to be comforted. He did not just trust to hearsay but sent the trusted Tychicus to help and support.

There was complete lack of suspicion as they all suffered for the sake and witness of Christ. Perhaps today our problem is that we are too comfortable and feel we can always meet our own needs. There is lack of doctrinal and spiritual unity, and everything has become fragmented because of the prevalence of the falsehoods and fake teachers that have infiltrated the church of Jesus Christ. There are names that name the Name but are not like the Name!

Paul was so like Christ that it was easy to trust him and what he said. He is vindicated by the Spirit of God and his word remains with us today. His first interest was the Christian people in the individual churches, and everyone could see it because of the kind of life he led. His sacrifice was as the obedience of Christ, who gave all for our sake.

Today, we have many who feather their own nests and take from the saints of God, leaving many in hardship while they live privileged and well provided-for lives. This should not be. We look out for ourselves and not the things of Christ or the struggling people of God. Church money is spent on fixtures and fitting and salaries and members suffer with low paid work and are barely able to meet the temporal needs of family. We have many ways to justify what we do, but there should be no gaps in the provision for each other in our church societies.

How much is spent on paying staff to do outreach? Why does everyone not work at a job to provide for their own needs, as the Apostle Paul did? Why is there one privileged person who must be supported by others to do "church work?" It has a negative impact on the fellowship and a disempowering effect on the body of believers.

Actual church members remain inadequate and unable to share with others the good news about Christ and the heavenly home. Our characters are suspect as we remain reticent and infants in reaching out to others, saints or sinners! We are passive recipients of talk that seems to go nowhere.

If Paul and Tychicus operated like we do today, the church would have died a long time ago. There is a distinct feeling of winding down and a terrible apathy about spiritual issues in too many places and in too many Christian lives. We are accountable and we are failing the younger generations. Predator leaders, prey on the flock of God, it is true, but the sheep allow it and appear spiritually gullible. It is a non-virtuous circle of lack of personal devotion and a dirth of sound doctrine being taught. The lack of both feeds on the failure that this produces, and our churches are reduced to social circles like the world, and just as unjust.

The preaching of the gospel is forgotten. Neither Saint nor sinner benefit from this and the church shrinks in every way. Leaders are desperate for money to keep going and so pander to the emotional needs, rather than the faithful preaching of the Word, another non-virtuous circle ensues. The Lord weeps. Paul would weep. We do not. Apathy reigns and our purpose is lost. What if Tychicus would visit us today? Who would he turn to, to help the churches of God? Each looks out for its own. We need the Lord Jesus to rescue us again from this present evil age. The sleeping saints need to awaken and search for God again, repent and turn from indolence and self-satisfaction. We need the honest and open preaching of the eternal Good News that transforms lives and turns our hearts to the Lord for good.

V9 Together

"...together with Onesimus, the faithful and beloved brother, who is one of you. They will make known to you everything that is going on here."

This Onesimus is also a brother with a godly character in Colosse who has the same vision as Paul and the Apostles. The Onesimus who is identified as a converted slave to Philemon who ran away and found himself with the Apostle Paul, could well be this person, but we do not really know. Whoever he was, he was a reliable servant of the gospel of Jesus Christ and has been given this trusted job to do in the church at Colosse.

This is not a one-way street of help or encouragement but is the sharing of the churches of God with each other. Paul is eager to know the news from Colosse but Tychicus and Onesimus will also relate to them the news from Paul. The closeness of the relationships in the New Testament churches is very touching and the levels of trust, are as is fitting in Christ.

Paul entrusts his work to these two brothers, and they are faithful to their dearly beloved brother Paul, who is in chains.

John Calvin maintains that it was not the runaway slave that is spoken about here, who he labels with a bad character, even though a converted brother! John Gill identifies the name Onesimus, with the slave of Philemon and tradition holds that he became a trusted and loyal servant of the early church.

Personally, I prefer the view of John Gill, since he ascribes change and personal holiness to the converted runaway slave and gives space for the grace of God in his life. What a great testimony that God will lift up those who are sinful and change them and make them what they are not, trustworthy and loyal. It is the same for us. We are all moral failures and under the wrath of a holy God, until we repent from our sinful mind and deeds and put our trust in the Saviour Christ. All those who have done mighty things for God are those who are clear about their natural status before God and always conscious of what they have been saved from. God will use the humility of the repentant sinner to do His work and the result will be great glory for His name.

There are some who will label people according to the multitude of their sins and the magnitude of their failures and exclude them for service and usefulness. This is a great pity and indicates the presence of some judgmental self-righteousness that is willing to keep people down and reminded them that they are failures and always to feel the effect of that. God does not operate in this way, but freely forgives and wipes out the remembrance of all sin from the record of the penitent sinner.

Paul himself was always conscious of his gross sins and therefore able to forgive the sinful failures, which is all of us! and include them in the work of the Lord. Paul calls Onesimus the faithful and beloved brother, and so he was – forgiven and lifted up to usefulness and a blessing to the church of Jesus Christ.

V10 Receive

"Aristarchus, my fellow prisoner, greets you, and Mark, the cousin of Barnabas (concerning whom you received commandments, "if he comes to you, receive him")"

Here is another godly brother mentioned who is a fellow prisoner with the Apostle Paul, in chains for the sake of Christ. He was involved with Paul in his many exploits for the faith, including being arrested at Ephesus. He was obviously a dear brother to Paul and Paul is keen that his greeting go to the saints at Colosse.

Also, Mark, otherwise called John Mark, which is striking as Mark disappointed the Apostle at one point in his life by going back from the ministry. After a fruitless mission, the young servant of the Lord is discouraged enough to leave the ministry and return home. Paul was disappointed by this weakness, and it caused an argument between Paul and Barnabas. Barnabas took John Mark with him in his ministry where he again proves himself. John mark is also the writer of the book of Mark and loves the Lord Jesus with all his heart. Now, Paul has forgiven and reinstated him into the ministry and in good faith.

Barnabas also is a contender for the faith and a faithful administrator in the church. Even though he had a sharp disagreement with the Apostle Paul, there is now no rancour, and the division has healed up and the characters involved have been changed and reunited by the Lord.

It is refreshing to reads the nuts and bolts of the relationships of these mighty men of God, who had differences that seemed to tear them apart, yet they were able to resolve their issues and unity in the gospel of the Lord Jesus Christ. Each has proved themselves as faithful servants of the Lord, but all having failures and misunderstandings as well. They are united in doctrine and faith and are all subject to the teaching of the scripture and therefore have all things in common. There is no theological divisions or arguments about the truth of God, for all are devoted to the Scripture and to the Lord. The Lord honours them with unity and peace. They support each other in the spread of the gospel and in the encouragement of the churches.

Paul is urging the Christians at Colosse to welcome all who come with Paul's blessing and commandment.

V11 Comfort

"...and Jesus who is called Justus. These are my only fellow workers for the Kingdom of God who are of the circumcision, men who have been a comfort to me."

Though these fellow workers mentioned here by Paul are his close confidants, labourers and suffering with him in the gospel, they are all of the circumcision, yet have given their lives over to the service of the Gentile believers. Their love is for the people of God and not just a sect that they could belong to. They view the church of Christ from the wide and inclusive perspective that all who believe are part of that kingdom and are precious together in the Lord. They have supported the Apostle Paul in his ministry to the Gentile people and stood with him against those who would keep out the chosen and elect people, who are not of Jewish descent, from the church of Jesus Christ.

They are a reliable body of close friends who have supported him and encouraged him in the service of the Lord, and he to them. They have all suffered together and this has been a bond that has kept them close and in touch with each other, especially in their spiritual lives.

The name Justus, synonymous with Jesus or Joshua, was common in Jewish circles and denoted a man especially given over to righteous living and holiness of life. Some has the suffix "the just" attached to their names afterwards to demonstrate in their lives that they were devoted to godly living and devoted to God.

These named Christians comforted the Apostle Paul with prayers, reading the Scripture, standing in for him and being a witness with him in the spread of the Gospel of Jesus the Christ. We are fortunate indeed if we have such support in our lives and Christian people who will stand with us and beside us. Nevertheless, when all desert us, we are never abandoned by our precious Lord Jesus, who is a constant and faithful companion and friend to His people.

Paul eventually felt the sting of rejection and isolation, but the Lord stood with Him in his difficulties when no one else was able. He speaks of this in his letter to another brother in the Lord, Timothy.

"At my first defence, no one stood with me, but everyone deserted me. May it not be charged against them. But the Lord stood by me and strengthened me, so that through me the message would be fully proclaimed, and all the Gentiles would hear it. So I was delivered from the mouth of the lion. And the Lord will rescue me from every evil action and bring me safely into His heavenly kingdom. To Him be the glory forever and ever. Amen."

2 Timothy 4:16-18

The message is everything. What happens to us is in the mercy of the Lord and the Lord will keep us when we are faithful to Him. We will find ourselves alone at times and in these days of great falling away, it is common, but the Lord stands with His people and will never leave us or forsake us...

V12 Striving

"Epaphras, who is one of you, a servant of Christ, salutes you, always striving for you in his prayers, that you may stand perfect and complete in all the will of God."

What a testimony to have about your character to have in the Holy Scriptures! Epaphras is a dedicated man of God who is given over to prayer for all the saints of God and included are the saints at Colosse. Epaphras supports the Apostle Paul in the spread of the gospel but is also one of the believers at Colosse. Maybe he is part of the congregation there, but certainly he is a brother in the faith, in the united and inclusive church of Jesus Christ. He is also a devoted servant of Christ, a man of God who loves God with all his heart, soul and strength. We know this because he is devoted to prayer for the saints and prays for the right things for them. Not for success and the blessings of this transient life, but for the complete will of God to be shown in their lives.

What is God's will for His people?

That we might stand perfect and complete before Him in love.

Epaphras was one such Christian. As he sought perfection and to be complete in Christ in his own life, so he also sought it for other brothers and sisters and prayed for the people in Colosse with real devotion. His prayers were constant and took much effort as he petitioned the Lord for the people he knew in the church. His preoccupation was the will of God, knowing that God is sovereign and therefore His will for each one of us is best. We resist His will to our detriment, and therefore we strive to enter into the reality of that perfect obedience that marked the life of our Saviour and Lord. It is also the mark of salvation in the life of Epaphras who serve the Lord Jesus with the full vigour of love.

What do we strive for?

Mostly we strive to live and to do our best and make our way in the world, but the striving here is in spiritual considerations which come first in the lives of these godly men.

"But seek first God's Kingdom, and his righteousness; and all these things will be given to you as well."

Matthew 6:33

Epaphras had his priorities right and has put the Lord first in his life and is reaping the spiritual wellbeing of that mindset. He lacks nothing and he has strength to serve others because the Lord honours his choice to put the kingdom first and not himself. Earthly considerations hold no weight for him, as he trusts in the Lord and works hard knowing that the reward waits for him in the coming kingdom of heaven, to which he belongs.

V13 Zeal

"For I testify about him, that he has great zeal for you, and for those in Laodicea, and for those in Hierapolis."

Paul is incredulous of the life and ministry of his friend Epaphras, due to his devotion to the Lord and His work in this world. Paul sees and hears that zeal even as Epaphras prays for the work of God and the Christian believers in the churches. Epaphras has a real and genuine zeal for the Lord which shows itself in all of his life. He loves the people of God and wants the pinnacle of spiritual life for each one of them. He is zealous for their spiritual growth and sanctification and most probably was active in bring many of them to Christ and in tutouring them in the way of the Lord.

Paul pays great attention to the prayers of Epaphras and recognises the depths of the work of God in his life. His life is full of the zeal of the Holy Spirit as was the life of our Lord Jesus.

"His disciples remembered that it was written, "Zeal for your house will eat me up."

John 2:17

As it is in Christ, the zeal for the service of the Lord has consumed Epaphras and it shows itself in his work for the Lord and in his prayers.

There were Christians in other places who also benefitted from the zeal of Epaphras. Laodicea and Hierapolis were towns nearby and many of them were also converts because of the labours and prayers of Epaphras. His scope was wide and not limited to one place or one group of people.

Epaphras was also in prison with Paul at that time, but Paul does not mention it here. Perhaps he thought the people would be so upset by the news, such was the godly regard and love that Epaphras enjoyed.

V14 Greet

"Luke, the beloved physician, and Demas greet you."

This is the same doctor Luke who wrote the gospel of Luke and also the Acts of the Apostles. He records his observations and research with great and knowledgeable accuracy and his words have been kept for us by the Holy Spirit as the word of God. He was a medical doctor and a healer and trained as a Greek historian. This would explain his attention to detail which helps us to date and contextualise other scriptures. His work covers more than a quarter of the New Testament, which makes him the chief writer of the document. Luke is clearly identified as a Gentile disciple and addresses the issues of the two camps in his writings.

He worked closely and travelled widely with Paul, as an evangelist and physician and perhaps attend to the Apostles needs, as he suffered from an ailment that Paul referred to as his "thorn in the flesh." It was perhaps as eye complaint.

"For I testify to you that, if possible, you would have plucked out your eyes and given them to me."

Galatians 4:15

Perhaps Luke attend Paul as he suffered with this disability and treated him for the difficulties it made for the Apostle. Luke was a trusted and dear friend and brother as well as a healer and was an up-close record keeper of many important events in the life of Christ and the Apostles. He was not just loved by Paul, but was known by this title, *"The beloved physician."* – not just a physician of the body but also of the soul. He is responsible for bringing many to faith in Christ and the building up of the saints in faith and love.

Demas is the same disciple who at one time deserted the ministry and the Apostle Paul because he wanted to follow the world and what it offered to him.

"for Demas left me, having loved this present world, and went to Thessalonica; Crescens to Galatia, and Titus to Dalmatia."

2 Timothy 4:10

Demas has been renewed and reinstated by the Apostle to his post in serving the Lord. It is for our blessing that these names are recorded here, that we may see the love of God at work in the lives of regular people like us with all their failings and mistakes. Some leaders are very strident in their judgement of those who fall and fail, and exclude people, who make mistakes and cause concern, but the Apostle Paul is so different. His human concern for all and his compassion for the person who fails is bourn out of his own sinfulness and the fact that he was the *"chief of sinners"* because he persecuted the church of God. God makes no mistakes in his Word, nor does he mistakenly give credence to the people who wrote it. The compassion of the Lord is not less than sinful people, and the fact that Demas is included here is a comfort to the saints of God.

V15 House

"Greet the brothers who are in Laodicea, and Nymphas, and the assembly that is in his house."

Paul asks that the Christians in Colosse also reach out and greet the brothers and sister in Laodicea, in his name. These two churches were sister churches and had fellowship together and much in common. They were both facing the onslaught of the effects of this fallen world on the minds of the believers and the attendant temptations to embrace the culture of the age. Laodicea is mentioned in Revelation chapter three and is a church that has become complacent and taken up with this world's goods and not the spiritual ways of the Lord. The letter to the Colossians is applicable to the Laodiceans also, and to us a well. Paul would not have known the full effect of his godly words on the readers, including us, but his words are the very Word of God.

Someone called Nymphas is singled out for mention, as the church also meets in his house. The believers met together often for fellowship, Bible sharing, sharing

these letters of Paul, and prayer and
singing. They could not long stay away
from each other and were very close in
their relationships with the Lord and each
other. People opened up their homes for
the spread of the gospel and Christian
fellowship.

We don't know if the church actual met in
the home of Nymphas, or small groups
met there, or another smaller fellowship in
another part of town. We know that the
believers had all thing common and
shared with each other in warm and loving
ways, and part of that was homes open to
the work of the Lord.

Perhaps it was a large godly family who
met together and operated like a church in
their street... Perhaps this is how they did
their outreach- families operating to the
glory of God and sharing the gospel openly
with all around them. Perhaps families
were functional witnesses to the grace of
God and bearing the likeness of Christ,
and showing His character to a lost world.

Whatever the actual circumstances, the
culture was one of openness, sharing and
warmth, and not just meeting to listen to
preaching once a week in a building that

was hardly used... it was a far cry from some of the situations that exist today.

V16 Among

"When this letter has been read among you, cause it to be read also in the assembly of the Laodiceans; and that you also read the letter from Laodicea."

The Christians were sharing the letters from the Apostle Paul with each other and learning the truths of God straight from his hand. Paul wrote the letter to be publicly read to the whole congregation of the church, and not to any one person in particular. The listeners did not realise they were designated to be in the canon of Scripture, but the truth in them resonated with the Holy Spirit who dwelt in each one of them. Paul does not hide from the Christians and teaches them the full council of God, pointing out their failure and weaknesses that they might grow in grace and turn from all evil.

The Christians placed great value on the Word of God. They read the Scriptures when they met together but did not always live accurately according to the precepts taught in them. Much like we do today, they appreciated, read and agreed but putting it into practice was more challenging. They were prone to false teachers and the wretched judaisers, who sought to dull down the message of the gospel and make it of no effect. Their difficulties were much the same as we face today, and the scripture is timeless in dealing with these recurring issues that follow the truth of God in every era.

We need the Scriptures at all times to strengthen our faith and the bonds we have with each other. Swapping letters was a great way to spread the Word, establishing it as the truth of God and ensuring that all the people were exposed to the gospel of Jesus Christ. The letters would have been copied and delivered to the other churches and thereby were spread through the country.

"These words, which I command you today, shall be on your heart; and you shall teach them diligently to your children, and shall talk of them when you sit in your house, and when you walk by the way, and when you lie down, and when you rise up. You shall bind them for a sign on your hand, and they shall be for frontlets between your eyes. You shall write them on the door posts of your house and on your gates."

Deuteronomy 6:6-9

Every time and place is good for the Word... let it be read among us...

V17 Heed

"Tell Archippus, "Take heed to the ministry which you have received in the Lord, that you fulfil it."

Paul now singles out a brother for a personal mention, presumably because Paul is concerned about the work he is doing, or not doing for the Lord. Archippus is a fellow worker with Paul and is in charge of the church in Colosse, as a minster of the gospel. He has been given this task to do, by the Lord, and must do it with all his heart and soul, and Paul is telling him here that he must get on with that task. His work is to preach the Word to the believer and the unbeliever alike, to teach the saints and preach the gospel of salvation from sin to the outsiders.

Perhaps Archippus was not so dedicated as he should have been and had lost some enthusiasm for the service of the Lord, which he had been entrusted with. He must find again his peace with God and put in the efforts necessary to fulfil his calling as a minister of the Lord Jesus. Paul says, "take an interest" and get your mind, hearts and body in gear for the work of the Lord. Archippus must defend the truth of God and teach the people against the error that is creeping into the congregation. This was a big problem and still is. We need ministers, who will faithfully hold on to the truths of God and preach them to the people, not people-pleasers who minister to itching ears, but someone who will stand for what is true in all circumstances.

We also must take the interest in the task that God has given us to do for His glory, whatever those tasks might be. It does not matter if no one sees us or pays any attention to what we do, we do it as unto the Lord and for the praise of His glory. We are to fulfil our calling and obey.

Maybe he is also encouraging the church to get behind their brother and help and support the ground-breaking ministry he is doing in the outreach for precious souls in the local community. Maybe he is telling the saints to make their minster more accountable to them and to help him to know that they are interested and behind what he should be doing. This also includes being interested enough to be involved and to put all their efforts behind the work of the Lord.

"Serve the LORD with gladness. Come before his presence with singing."

Psalm 100:2

We serve with all our hearts and soul. We hold back nothing from the one who died for us and gave everything to save us.

Beloved, let us encourage each other in the work of the Lord, as He has assigned it to us...

V18 Remember

"The salutation of me, Paul, with my own hand: remember my bonds. Grace be with you. Amen."

Paul says goodbye to the Christians at Colosse with a heavy heart, for he knows he will not see them again on this side of eternity. He signs the letter with his own hand, for he has written it in the straights of prison, and there were also many imposters. The best thing he can leave with the believers, is to confer the grace of God unto them. This is the greatest blessing in the Christians life – to have the work of the Holy Spirit within us and ministering to our souls. His grace to us is wonderful in the extreme and appreciated by those who walk closely with Him.

Touchingly, Paul reminds the believers that He is in prison and to not forget what he is facing every day. He is in prison for the cause of Christ and for speaking out the gospel to so many in a myriad of circumstances. He has carried the burden for them that they might be taught the truths of God and be guided on all truth. He is asking them to pray for him and to not forget him. It so easy to forget those who are out of the circle of our friends and acquaintances, and we can be so hard-hearted about those who are alone in their lives. Some blamed the Apostle for his circumstances, saying he had surely sinned grievously and was being chastised, one of the many discouragements Paul must have faced in that dreadful place. Although in chains, he remains content in the Lord and continually gives of himself for the believers.

It must have been so difficult for the Apostle Paul as he faced the loneliness and the threat of death as he sat in a prison cell. He is humble and still asks for prayer that he might be sustained.

Still, he is labouring for the Lord, and remembering the saints in all the churches that he has had input into, and cares for them all so deeply. He asked them to remember him, and not forget him. He is in this position for their sake and deserving of sympathy and care.

"Remember those who are in bonds, as bound with them; and those who are ill-treated, since you are also in the body."
Hebrews 13:3

His final words are full of the grace of God and the agreement of the Holy Spirit that the Colossian Christians and all who will read this letter will be filled with grace. So also we, in these last days enjoy the benefits of this great epistle. I also pray the Word will dwell in you richly and bear eternal fruit and that this book is an encouragement to you.